MITHRAIC MYSTERIES

RESTORED AND MODERNIZED

A DRAMA OF INTERIOR INITIATION

Employing all the available Data and Survival of the Historic Persio-Roman Mithraics embodying versions of Zoroastrian Scriptures combining the Religions of all Races and Times, with the best of Modern Spiritual Thought with Experiments for every Day of the Year.

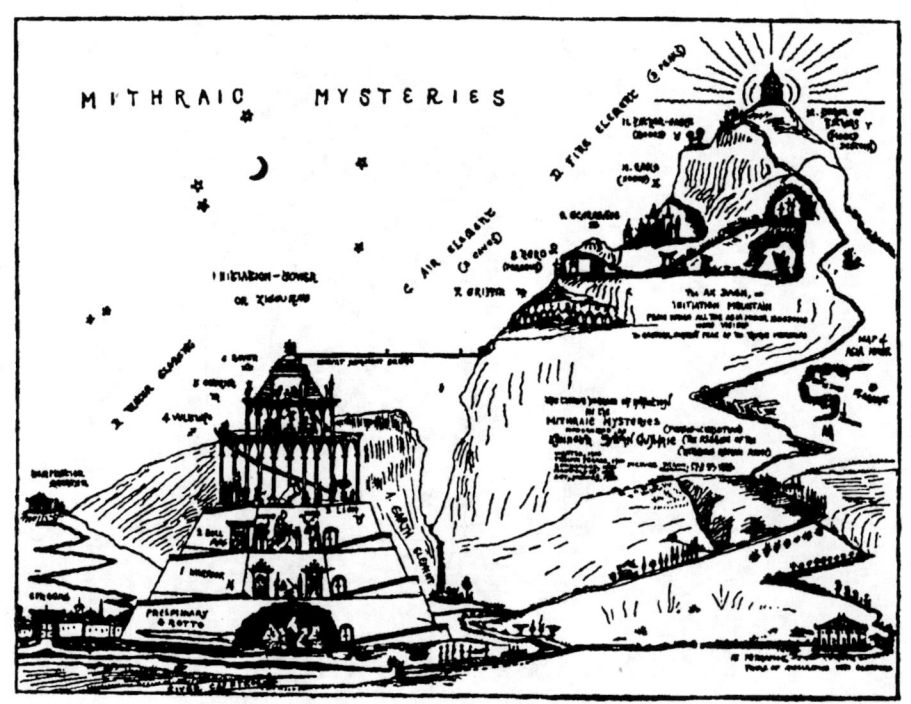

Kenneth Sylvan Guthrie

ISBN 1-56459-366-5

Request our FREE CATALOG of over 1,000

Rare Esoteric Books

<u>Unavailable Elsewhere</u>

Alchemy, Ancient Wisdom, Astronomy, Baconian, Eastern-Thought, Egyptology, Esoteric, Freemasonry, Gnosticism, Hermetic, Magic, Metaphysics, Mysticism, Mystery Schools, Mythology, Occult, Philosophy, Psychology, Pyramids, Qabalah, Religions, Rosicrucian, Science, Spiritual, Symbolism, Tarot, Theosophy, *and many more!*

Kessinger Publishing Company
Montana, U.S.A.

Kenneth Sylvan Guthrie

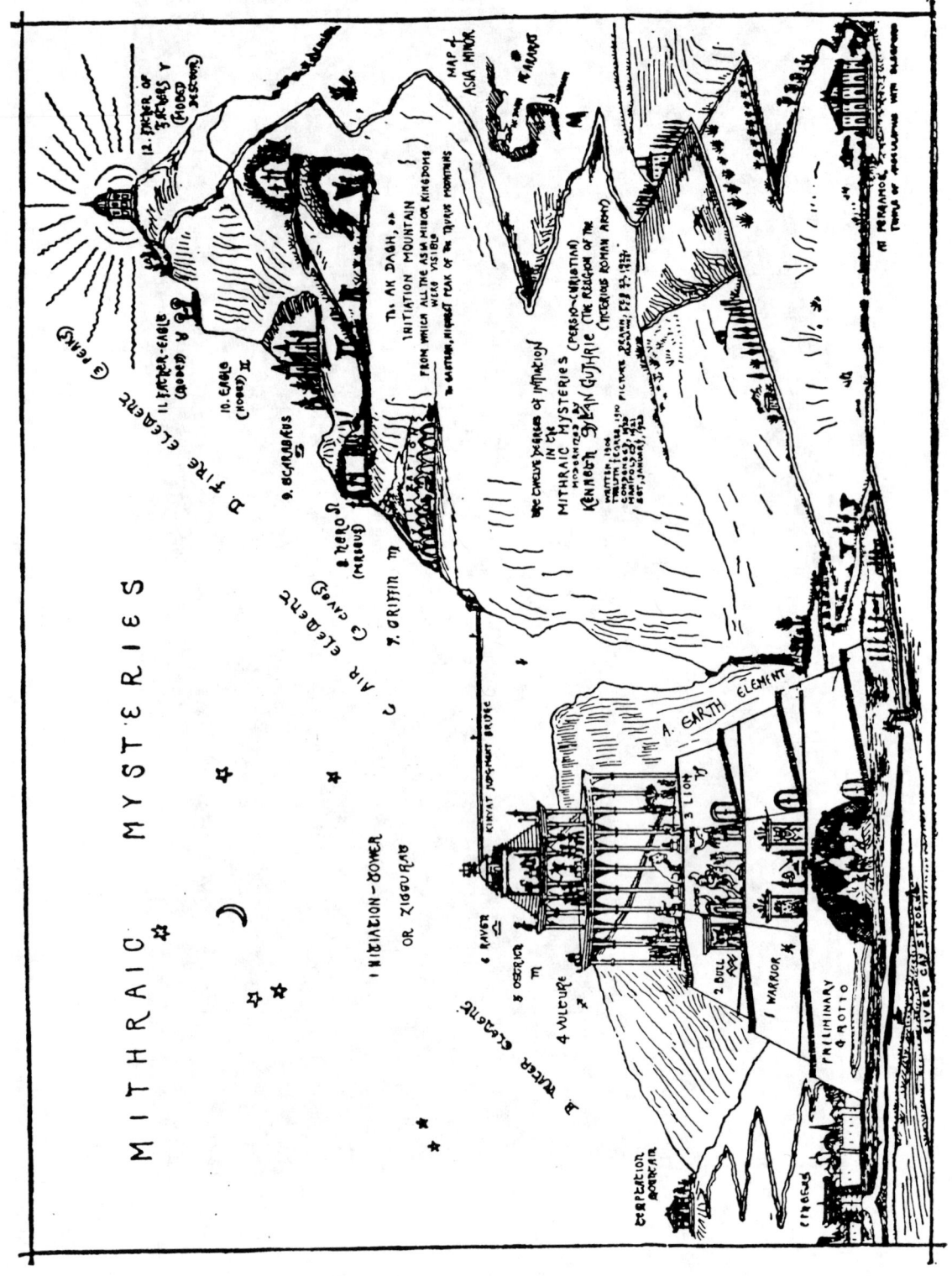

General Outline of the
Mithraic Mysteries, Modernized

Introduction,

Reception of Neophytes,   Temptation

First Three Degrees, on the Earth.

1	Warrior,	Search for Truth
2	Bull,	Control of Sleep
3	Lion,	Achievement of Health

Second Three Degrees, through Water.

4	Vulture,	Comparative Religion
5	Ostrich,	Valuation of Error
6	Raven,	Judgment of Self-knowledge

Reached by the Kinvat Bridge,
Third Three Degrees, in the Air.

7	Griffin,	Vindication of Divine Justice
8	Persian Hero,	Calling of the Saviors
9	Scarabeus,	Building of Sanctuaries

Last Three Degrees, in Supernal Fire.

10	Eagle,	Soul-Marriage to Wisdom
11	Father,	Choice of Successors
12	Supreme Father,	Unveiling of Final Truth

Historical.

The *Mithraic Mysteries* are an adaptation of the later Zoroastrian Mithras cult in the Roman Empire. *Mithras* means *Friend* or *Mediator;* he was the god of light, solar, and spiritual, and consequently mysteries of his would constitute *enlightenment.* For 1200 years it was the official cult of the Persian kingdom, and it is said that on those feast-days alone the Persian kings enjoyed the questionable privilege of intoxication. On clearing the Mediterranean Sea of corsairs, Pompey's soldiers were initiated into it, brought it back home, and made it the official religion of the Roman Army, which in turn carried it all over Europe, as far as Scotland. This entailed the building of thousands of chapels, called *mithraeums* all over Europe and Asia, one particularly famous one being at *Heides*heim near Frankfurt.

Probably to increase their influence with their soldiers, several Emperors were initiated, and its chief festivals were publicly celebrated in Rome, Mithra's birth-day on the 25th of December, and the *Hierocorax* festival. This public entrenchment could alone explain why the Western Church split from the Eastern Church rather than accept the historically Christian Epiphany and Quadragesiman Easter, and why the Sabbath changed to *Sunday*, and its official imperial adoption; also why there were so many Christian officers, such as Sebastian and Martin of Tours.

Mithraism practised a baptism and a communion with elements made of water and flour, and it stressed the ideals of friendship, purity, manliness, woman's equality, & zodiacal character-training.

Its similarity to Christianity was so marked, and also so unignorable that Tertullian claimed that it had been invented by the Devil, as a counterfeit of Christianity. This however would be an anachronism, as Mithraism is the older by 500 years. On the other hand Dupuis, judging from some of the facts mentioned above, looks on Christianity as Judaized Mithraism: but fortunately we need not decide the question, as Mithraism was suppressed in 348, on the establishment of its Christian variety.

A surviving liturgy was published by Dietrich, and has been incorporated here, along with Apollonius's *Nuktemeron*, and much from Zoroastrian sources. In this poetical form it is hoped that all good elements of all good sources have been retained.

Layard reproduced the monumental relics, and Blake, in his *Evolution of Morality* expounded them. Francis Cumont reduced the Degrees to seven, and in the *Monist* Phythian-Adams had some interesting articles.

Biographical.

In my career the winter 1905-1906 was wasted. Interrupting my life-work to devote my energies to an independent philosophical group in New York, I received neither compensation, time to produce my own works, nor gratitude. My business advice having been scorned, the naturally resulting misfortunes were blamed on me. My self-respect then drove me out overnight pennyless into the unknown, to start a new life, leaving them to the ruin deserved by their self-will, and failure to appreciate devoted service. From the wreck the only thing saved was the draft of these Mysteries, made at lost moments at top speed, and read to a sympathetic friend, Miss Elizabeth Cornell, at the Fort in Central Park. She most kindly helped me by type-writing them.

As has happened with other Mystic rituals, the supreme Degrees were the weakest, and shortest. The last three were accordingly rewritten, the Twelfth demanding the whole summer of 1909 in Philadelphia, in the sunny upper back room of Miss Elizabeth Fracker, a lady whose hospitality protected me during the years in which I had risked my all to devote myself to interior development.

Even the first complete copy was not put together till Nov. 1913—Jan. 1914, while Assistant at the Church of the Holy Apostles. A second copy was put together in separate volumes on Nov. 6, 1917 under the encouragement of that prominent Scottish Rite leader, Mr Hall, of Nashville.

Originally the Degrees were written to follow the initiation experiences of twelve candidates, each representing one of the twelve chief types of character, making these Degrees a treatise of cosmic value, a school of spiritual development for every living being. It was magnificent and colossal, — only too much so! Their length condemned them, first for a magazine, *the Word*, that had begun to publish them, and then so much the more for myself. Still the manuscript is there, ready for publication, in the event of the means being provided by some interested friend. — Therefore despairing of publication in its original form, I cut down the twelve characters to two initiates, one male representing the head, and one female, representing the heart. This was done in July 1918, during a flying trip to the Church Summer School at Geneva, N.Y., while I was trying to place in book-stores my novel, the *Romance of Two Centuries*.

After securing a possible text, I had to decide on a method of production, and my humility and despair were satisfied with a Duplicator. At a parting communion with my friend Ernest Laycock, in September 1919 I was from within shown how to produce the work in different-sized pamphlets with suggestions and experiments such as to adapt the Degrees to practical use by correspondence. But in May 1922 after completing the setting of my New Testament and Angelic Mysteries, I was after prayer shown that they would reach a wider audience if set, which I accordingly completed by Thanksgiving 1922.

Enemies of my accomplishing anything at all have accused me of impatience; but it seems to me this record of sixteen years' persistence is a sufficient refutation of that charge.

Mere printing and circulation have however never been the limit of my aspirations. My Community efforts in Oak Lane in 1900-1903 had really been inspired by the dream of a modernization of the ancient Mysteries; but this was brought to a close by my betrayal by a friend. Later I tried to satisfy this craving by joining the Scottish Rite in Brooklyn; but here also I was doomed to spiritual disappointment. For me there was nothing left but *to initiate myself by writing my own Mysteries.*

This craving for Mysteries with its literary results was no fluke or accident. Whether or not I had been initiated in some Mysteries during some former incarnation, I do not know; but this I do know, that as an eleven-year old boy in 1882, in our library in Wiesbaden, I would throw myself on the floor in agonies of tears, uttering three prayers, to know the true facts underlying the traditional life of Jesus, to learn the ancient Mysteries, and to live the life of a Galahad. All this was obscured by travels, studies and self-support; and it was only thirty years later, on completion of these Mithraic Mysteries, that that scene flashed back on my mind, with the realization that I had unconsciously myself fulfilled those prayers by my New Testament studies, my Mithraic Mysteries, and my Regeneration books. Thus had I predestined myself: and I wonder whether *coming events cast their shadows before,* or *are prayers answered?* Perhaps both.

This work had an unexpected sequel in the *Angelic Mysteries* which I wrote after a revelation on St Michael & All Angels' in 1918, and the *Modern Mysteries*, planned in the summer of 1921, but which I will never have the strength to carry out.

INTRODUCTION.
SCENE I.
The Presentation of the Neophytes.
(Porter locking the Gate. A knock is heard.)

PORTER:
Another one?

MYSTA:
(From without)
If it be not too late!

PORTER:
Almost; but I will open once again.
Come in! But wear this mask, the both of you;
(Enter Mystus, Dives and Mysta, putting on the mask.)
The Mask of Holy Aspirations. Thus
Your former lives, vicissitudes and griefs
Shall be left behind at this high gate: —
Here all are neophytes, or priests of truth.

(Mystus and Dives advance among the crowd, who are speaking to each other in small groups. As the gates close and are locked, knocking is heard, several times; but the Porter repeatedly answers, "Too late." Faint music is heard; the inner gates open and there advances a procession of priests, with the Father of Mithras among them. They form a double line reaching to the gate. Those in front spread out into a circle, leaving only room for one at a time to enter between them. The Father of Mithras, with two priests at his side, stands in the circle. After a solemn chant has died away, the hierophant addresses the neophytes, who have grouped themselves in front of the stage, on both sides, profile to audience, facing him.)

HIEROPHANT:
Welcome, ye neophytes, within this fane,
This marvel of the human mind and skill.
But greater marvels are we now to do:
Of you we are to make divinities.

But each of you, before he enters, must
Declare what motives have inspired his choice.
Yourselves shall be your judges, whether you
Deserve the struggle for immortal joys.
Ye initiators, bring your neophytes;
Conduct them hither, one by one, to me.
   (An Initiator, with a blue robe and mask, leads on a youth.)
HIEROPHANT:
Welcome, my son! Declare thou unto us,
What thou wouldst have from us, thy soul's
   true friends?
NEOPHYTE:
I would have knowledge of the Gods and men.
HIEROPHANT:
That may'st thou have, if thou have eyes to see.
Who sent thee here?
NEOPHYTE:
Myself.
HIEROPHANT:
Then take thou heed
That thou forget not others as the end and aim
Of holy living. Tell us what at first
Aroused thy wish to pass these mysteries?
NEOPHYTE:
I always read about them; and I thought
That I would find out for myself their truth.
HIEROPHANT:
What say ye, priests, shall we admit this man?
   (After a silence, the chief priest having consulted with the others.)
Yea, let him enter in the mysteries.
   (The hierophant takes a torch, lights it from a brazier, and gives it to the neophyte.)
Henceforth, thy name among us this shall be:
Mystus, proceed, and victory be thine!

MODERNIZED MITHRAIC MYSTERIES

(The initator takes the neophyte in turn to seven priets who stand around in a circle. The first, dressed in a silver-colored starred mantle, and wearing anklets, bids the neophyte put his foot on the block, and puts anklets on him. The second, dressed in a yellow starred mantle, and wearing bracelets, bids the neophyte extend his hands, and puts bracelets on them. The third, dressed in a blue starred robe, and wearing a girdle, endues him with a girdle. The fourth, dressed in a red starred robe, and wearing a breast pin, places one on his garment. The fifth, dressed in an orange starred robe, and wearing ear pendants, puts some on him. The sixth, dressed in a black starred mantle and wearing a necklace, hangs one around his neck. The seventh, dressed in a gold starred mantle, and wearing a crown, places one on his head.)

(Mysta comes on, a woman.)

HIEROPHANT:
Welcome, dear daughter! What desirest thou?

NEOPHYTE:
I crave from you the power to make my way.

HIEROPHANT:
That mayest thou have, if that thy way be right.
Therefore, which is the way of thy desires?

NEOPHYTE:
I would have power to charm and fascinate.

HIEROPHANT:
That mightst thou have, if those that thou
  wouldst charm
And fascinate, were holy, wise and good.
Who are they thou wouldst charm and
  fascinate?

NEOPHYTE:
Him who just now went out. Refuse me not!
I am sincere; make any sacrifice —
Nay, life itself, to gain my little end.
I will be faithful, do you do with me
Whate'er you please; but let me also go.

HIEROPHANT:
My child, thou knowest not that which thou wish'st.
Hast thou reflected that thy lover will
Have changed in passing through the mysteries?

NEOPHYTE:
Then I would also change. I will fulfill
The least of stipulations that you make;
But let me pass, and I will do your will.

HIEROPHANT:
Who sent thee here?

NEOPHYTE:
'Twas he: he said to me
"I go — farewell! Unless thou, too, wilt come."
And then I thought that if he went, I, too,
Would make the attempt — if me he should forget
I would be also changed, forgetting him.
No doubt I know not what I ask from you;
But can I offer more than all my life?

HIEROPHANT:
What say ye, priests? Shall we admit this child?

PRIESTS:
Yea, let her enter in the mysteries;
If so her love for him be greater than
Her love for her own safety and her wealth,
She shall not see him any more until
She have become incapable of ill.

HIEROPHANT:
Thou hearest, daughter, is it so with thee?

NEOPHYTE:
'Tis so, and shall be so with me, henceforth.

HIEROPHANT:
(Handing her a lighted torch.)
Henceforth thy name among us this shall be:
Mystal. Go in, and victory be thine!
(The neophyte is endued with jewels, as above.)
(Dives comes on.)
HIEROPHANT:
Welcome, my son! Fear not to let us know
What thou wouldst have from us, thy soul's true friends?
NEOPHYTE:
Whatever you may have to give to me.
HIEROPHANT:
I asked thee, son, what thou desir'dst of us:
Each man receives the special gift he craves.
NEOPHYTE:
I came for initiation, like the rest.
HIEROPHANT:
Then thou dost not desire some special gift?
NEOPHYTE:
I think I have all that the world can give;
What more could I receive from obscure priests?
HIEROPHANT:
Who sent thee here?
NEOPHYTE:
My interest in you.
I've visited the temples everywhere,
And to support the worship left rich gifts.
HIEROPHANT:
In vain, my son, thou laborest for them,
In vain thou visitest the various shrines,
And thinkest what thou mayest do for them;
Far rather look for what thou mayest receive
Now tell me what at first aroused thy wish
For initiation in the mysteries?

NEOPHYTE:
I do not know — if not to visit them,
And all their shattered temples to rebuild —
To have priests pray for me, so that my name
Might be continued after I am dead.
HIEROPHANT:
Hast thou e'er hear the truth? Desir'st thou it?
NEOPHYTE:
Most certainly, or I had not come here.
I would be glad to get what truth you have;
But when your temples shall have been
 rebuilt. . . .
HIEROPHANT:
Now leave the temples, and confine yourself
Unto the issues of your own weak soul.
Are you of those who talk of it at times,
Of principle, of righteousness, of truth,
As if they were something subsidiary
Unto the glorifying of yourself?
What think ye, priests? Shall we admit this
 man
Unto the worship of our mysteries?
PRIESTS:
Not yet! Probation must he undergo.
HIEROPHANT:
Thou hearest what they say: — Probation first.
NEOPHYTE:
I did not hear correctly what you said.
Probation? Me! Who visit all the globe,
The friend of governors — e'en emperors?
And you admitted here, two commoners
While me, the gentleman, you would *probate?*
Me, who have promised to rebuild your shrine?
Impossible.

MODERNIZED MITHRAIC MYSTERIES

HIEROPHANT:
My son, refrain thyself.
Thyself hast ratified the priests' decree.
When thou hast learn'd the lesson thou'lt be taught
Within the schoolroom of the neophytes,
The lesson of supremacy of truth,
The primacy of principle and right,
O'er all considerations possible,
Then mayest thou come again into this hall,
And mayest receive from me thy lighted torch.
Next year! till then, farewell, my wayward son.

NEOPHYTE:
This serves me right, for lowering myself
Unto these priests of questionable fame!
I will not stay a year — I will go home,
And never more demean myself to them.

HIEROPHANT:
My son, thy bitterness will do thee harm,
Far more than us. Why not accept defeat
In the same spirit it is forced on thee,
The keeping of a worthy standard here,
That thou mayest learn a nobler attitude?
Be humble! Learn! And come again to us,
And thou shalt find thy year's delay a gain.
Among us here there is no rivalry:
The erring most, we love, and honor most
Those who were great enough to understand
Their imperfections, and who set to work
To turn a weakness into source of strength.
My son, I know thee rich in this world's goods,
And though the temples moulder and decay,
Until thou comest humbly for the truth,
Not one sesterce will we accept from thee,

Whose soul is starving in thy worldly cares.
Behold, my son, I will be generous,
And will make use, for thee, of thy best self.
Dost thou desire to help us?

NEOPHYTE:

Certainly.

HIEROPHANT:

Then, not to save thyself, but just for this,
To give us help, pray alter thine own self,
Enable us to accept a gift from thee —
For we receive no gifts but from our own.
My son, return not to thy worldly life;
Stay in the outer temples for this year,
And make thee worthy of thy better self.
Thou wilt remain?

NEOPHYTE:

I will, O hierophant, —
For thou hast conquered me by wisdom's love,
And I am proud to have been overcome
By thee. I will remain, and fit myself
To be real service unto you.
Farewell!

(With tears in his eyes, priests conduct him out by door to right.)

(Suddenly a masked figure steps up and bars the way for the neophytes toward the gate at the back and cries out in rough tones:)

FIGURE:

Beware, ye neophytes! Consider well!
Beware, I say: the path is dangerous!

MYSTUS:

And is that all? Then stand aside! I go!

MYSTA:

The world we leave is also dangerous.

MODERNIZED MITHRAIC MYSTERIES 13

FIGURE:
Beware, I say! Entrance is not refused,
But know the risks before you enter here.
You yet can go back home, and be content.
When you have learnt the truth, to fail is sin,
And your own better selves your jailors are.
Never again will you permit yourselves
To enjoy the blessings that before were yours.
Physical sickness will avenge relapse,
And you yourselves will not permit yourselves
To leave your Hell until you have attained.
Better return, unless your minds are firm!
Return to home, and wealth, and friends, with
　　health.
Yet, all the willing may attempt the path!
Are you?

MYSTUS:
I dare. I die without the truth.

FIGURE:
Are you?

MYSTA:
Divinity is destiny!
　(The figure turns and beckons to others similarly clad, who rush in and with cords, behind their backs, bind the neophytes' wrists, reviling them. They are horrified, and by gesture appeal to the hierophant, who, however, by kindly glances, encourages them. As the priests sing the following chorus, the initiates are by the figures, driven in, while the priests march on either side, into the portal that is at the back of the stage. The opened portal shows a glimpse of a temple scene.)

PRIEST'S CHORUS.
Hear with your ears what is best, perceive with
　your minds what is purest,

So that each man for himself may, before the great doom cometh,
Choose the creed he prefers. May the wise ones be on our side!
These two Spirits are twins: they made known in times that are by-gone
That good and evil, in thought, and word, and action,
Rightly decided between them the good; not so the evil.
When these two came together, first of all they created
Him who was kind and good, whose robe was the changeless heaven,
Chose what was right; these, too, whose works pleased Ahura-Mazda.
But to the good came Might; and with Might came Wisdom and Virtue;
Armaiti herself, the eternal gave to their bodies
Vigor; e'en thou wert enriched by the gifts that she scattered, O Mazda.
They could not rightly discern who erred, and worshipped the Devas;
They chose the Bad Spirit and having held counsel together,
Turned to Rapine, that so they might make man's life an affliction.
O Men, if you but cling to the precepts Mazda has given,
Precepts, which to the bad are torment, but joy to the righteous,
Then shall you one day find yourselves victorious through them!

INTRODUCTION.
SCENE II.

(The peak of Ak Dagh, the mountain-temple of Aesculapius, near Pergamos. On a lower peak is seen the temple itself, with visiting throngs; snatches of music are heard. It is high noon, and the heat is sultry on the top, in spite of occasional breezes. The neophytes, in dust-stained white robes are seated about in small groups, taking advantage of every small shade. Mystus is at the summit, under the shadow of a stone. The noon-trumpets from below are heard, and he awakes from a reverie, and looks down first at the temple, and then turns westward to the ocean, whose horizon can be seen.)

MYSTUS:
Not here, but there — thither my heart now turns,
To worship, at this solemn hour, the Lord.
Thou sun of heaven and of human souls,
I worship thee, here on this lonely peak,
And join my prayers with my dear ones at home
Where now the choric hymn to thee ascends.
God give me strength of will to persevere!
Fainter, my spirit looks upon this scene,
Dizzily glancing at this broad expanse.
Send help — since help comes after all from Thee.

(Eschem, a demon, appears in the guise of a priestess of the temple of Aesculapius. She climbs up the rock in time to hear the last cries of Mystus. She seems kind and motherly.)

ESCHEM:
I see I come in time to bring thee help.
I have in Ephesus, a boy like thee,
And when each day I saw thee suffering here,
From down below, the temple, while at my prayers,

I thought my soul was calling me to thee.
Thy time is over — on the fortieth day.
Here is refreshment for the heart and mind,
It is not food, — thou didst not ask for it,
Although hadst thou come to the temple gates,
We had gladly given to thee a bite
To help thee fast unto the very end.
Only a fig or two, a little cake,
And if thou take it, it will seem to me
My boy at Ephesus will look more bright.
Here, sit down near me, my darling child,
And take this temporary stimulant.
(Mystus has betrayed by his features and actions how nearly the food has attracted him; but at the last moment he draws away and says reverently:)
O sacred priestess, blessings on thy head,
That thou hast brought this touching charity
To me, the helpless sufferer, up here.
Forgive me, if I seem irreverent,
Refusing these thy gifts of figs and cakes.
The promise that we neophytes did make
For forty days to abstain from every food
Will not elapse until yon sun has set.
Not matter of mere choice is it for me;
My promise was a law unto myself.
We grow diviner by conforming flesh
Unto the principles our soul has made.
Successful will-tasks discipline the soul
So that we live, not by mere bread alone
But by each word the Lord speaks forth through us.
And while no doubt the priests would not object
My taking comfort from thy reverent hands,

I would be ashamed because the law I made
Whereby to show the flesh I was its lord
I had not carried out unto the end.
Forgive thou my presumption, blessed one.

ESCHEM:
(Laying aside the food brought up.)
Do as thou wishest, faithful neophyte.
Yet continence up here no virtue is, —
Up here, where no temptations touch the sense;
But perfect is the victor who descends
Among temptations and remains untouched,
To be among the world, yet, not of it.
Written it is God's angel-messengers
Will guard your way from every accident.
Come down, and make thy victory complete!
I see in you my son, and for his sake,
I wish you made yourself the perfect man.
(By his gestures, Mystus has shown that he has become anxious and uncertain.)

MYSTUS:
Forgive me, lady dear and reverend,
If I again refuse your proferred help.
I would not tempt the Lord, considering
I have been fortunate in standing firm
Until the present moment, though up here.
From more temptation, Lord, deliver us!

ESCHEM:
O faithful child! How happy then must be
The mother of a son as wise as you!
Now that your forty days of fasting end
You dare to look around you: for behold
From hence, as from no other mountain top
May one behold the whole enlightened world:

The fifteen kingdoms of the Asian Land.
A glorious spectacle! and blessed you
Who having conquered saintship by this fast
Shall be enabled to assume the best
Of offices you may elect to take.
The neophyte achieving third degree
May have the choice of what he cares to do.
Immortal victors! Happy youth are you
To have discovered how to reach success!
All this fair world beneath your feet is yours,
As soon as you have carried out your vows.
Faint not! Support the temporary pain
Of hunger, thirst, of water, cold and heat,
So shall you be enabled to possess
All this brave world that waits for you, its lord!

MYSTUS:

Cease, priestess! and let me struggle here
Without the added fight with worldliness.
I swear by heaven that I came for truth!
I turn my gaze from these sublimest lands
Unto the untroubled skies, where hidden stars
Remind me of the angels all around.
Leave me alone! Depart! or I will flee!
   (With gestures of motherly grief, Eschem departs, calling:)
Farewell, my son, I grieve to leave thee so!

MYSTUS:

How skilfully she probed my troubled heart!
All that she said had found an echo there —
All that she said a thousand times I fought!
And then to hear her say it lovingly,
Made all those voices seem so sane and wise.
I nearly doubted my own sanity.

MODERNIZED MITHRAIC MYSTERIES

Prayer must be sane; I will find my refuge there
And look nowhere but at the setting sun.

(The same trumpet used in the reception of the neophytes is heard approaching. Mystus hears it, recognizes it, but closes his ears, and prays. Finally the Archimage appears, and taps them on the shoulder. Mystus looks up, recognizes him, springs up with joy, and reverently addresses him.)

MYSTUS:
How camest thou here, O reverend Archimage?

ARCHIMAGE:
We came to end your fast of forty days,
To give you food and drink, and take you all
To where you may begin the forty nights
Of perfecting, up here so well begun.
I see the demon Eschem has been here:
The untasted food!

MYSTUS:
The demon Eschem? What?
A temple-priestess said she that she was.

ARCHIMAGE:
Of course he said so; had he shown himself
In all his lurid trappings, you had fled.

(The archimage stamps on the basket of food, which disappears, leaving a small cloud of smoke.)

MYSTUS (bitterly):
That leaves no doubt of what she really was.
Thank God I did not get that smoke in me!

(He crosses himself. The archimage smiles indulgently. Mystus goes on:)

Where is the other sister neophyte?

ARCHIMAGE:
Stay here, one more will come. Thy instinct chose
The gathering place, nearest to heaven here.

(Initiator and initiatress enter, leading in the faint and dusty Mysta.. Temple servants bring food and drink, wash their feet, put on new sandals, new robes, and after a considerable time they gather around the archimage, who speaks as follows:)

ARCHIMAGE:
Let us in silence utter thanks to God!
            (A long silence.)
That neither neophyte is absent now.
My children, you have fasted forty days,
You have stood fast; wherefore you now proceed
To cave telestic of the mystic rites.
There must you suffer now for forty nights.
Then shall you crucify yourselves upon
The cross of water, fire, air and snow,
Until you stand within your realms supreme
And fit to enter through baptismal waves
Into the lustral land of mysteries,
Where with your eyes you shall behold the truth.
Wherefore be strong, for you will need your strength.
Do not despair when suffering on the cross.
For many have before you passed this way —
Lord Mithra, too. How else, do you suppose,
Did he attain to be redeemer of the race
But that he won his rank the first of all
Through full obedience to the lustral law?
Twice forty days the Saviour suffered thus;
And when you too, have gained the victory,
You then may look for immortality!
  (Silence, they all go out, Mystus and Mysta accompanied by an intiator of the opposite sex.)

FIRST DEGREE

𝔗𝔥𝔢 𝔚𝔞𝔯𝔯𝔦𝔬𝔯

The Centaur, and the Amazon.

The Mithraic Mysteries, Modernized.

First Degree, the Warrior, (Centaur & Amazon)

Major Points

1 **Symbol**, The Warrior: Centaur and Amazon.
2 **Purpose**, Search for Truth.
3 **Scene**, A grotto, deliverance from which is found, not by groping externally, but by listening internally.
4 **Peculiarity**, The means of escape is different for each person.
5 **Temptation**, To receive a crown from a sword.
6 **Oath**, To follow the Truth, and fight not men, but error only.
7 **Gift**, Spiritual Armor.

Minor Points

1 **Element**, Earth.
2 **Sign**, Pisces, or Feet.
3 **Planet**, Moon.
4 **Color**, Grey.
5 **Flower**, A crown of Papyrus Bloom.
6 **Jewel**, Anklets.
7 **Token**, Branding on forehead.

FIRST DEGREE

The Warrior, — Search for Truth

(A dark grotto, from which lead paths in several directions. From the central one glimmers a light, carried by *Mystus,* who who is weary and dusty. He is wearing seven amulets: anklets, girdle, bracelets, rings, a wreath around the chest, necklace, earrings and tiara. The same ornaments are worn by *Mysta,* when she appears later.)

Mystus, Since I am lost, I might as well proceed!
    (*Entering.*) A hall! Saved! Praise to God! These many paths
    Prove that I have progressed, and shall find light!
        (Examining the hall.)
  Alas, it is the self-same cave I left!
        (Sinks down wearily.)
    Exhausted, further efforts I resign!
    As well as elsewhere, here let Death approach!
Some person comes! Has Doom my challenge heard?
(He hides behind a rock. *Mysta,* bearing a small light, dragging herself, arrives through another passage.)

Mysta, Unto the very end I struggle on;
    And even ending, still shall I protest;
    This, my response unto unequal Gods!

Mystus, (aside,) A fellow-wanderer in terrestrial gloom,
    And one in straits more sore than are my own!
    This will afford the opportunity
    To play at Providence: still can I serve,
    And therefore live; and hoping, be redeemed!

28 FIRST, *WARRIOR*

(To her.) Fear not! I am a comrade, as it seems!

Mysta, (reassured,) I thank you, comrade, for your
But all I need is respite short, and rest. [kindliness.
    Meanwhile we may reflect on our mischance
    In this our individual search for Truth.
    These vain excursions only leading back
    Unto the starting-point, our only hope
    Must lie in method wholly different
    From search material, which we have **disproved**.
        (The Neophytes' lights go out.)

Mystus, Release must then be found within ourselves!

Mysta, By guessing the event's significance....

Mystus, With perseverance wise unto the end.

Mysta, Maybe these rocky walls are not so hard
    As is our blindness and stupidity!

Mystus, Of freedom we must earn our worthiness
    Before the hinges of the gates of Darkness turn.

Mysta, Let us in prayerful silence meditate
    How we enlightenment may yet achieve!

(After a momentary silence in the darkness, there is heard from *Mysta* suppressed laughter; she fumbles a little; then occurs an explosion with smoke. When this has cleared away, she has disappeared, but from a distance is heard in muffled tones)

Mysta, I have attained to freedom; follow me!

    (*Mystus* remains puzzled for a long period, but finally)

Mystus, The way she found to escape this maze of
Shall not lie hid from me; here was her seat: [doubt
    To follow, I must do what she has done.
    I saw her press somewhat behind that rock.

(*Mystus* gropes all around, pressing with his hands; it is in vain; he is discouraged.

    I see that though I also must escape,
    My exit must take place by other path.
    Of what she did what I must imitate

FIRST, *WARRIOR* 29

Is not so much the action she performed
As is the way she learned the freeing deed.
She listened carefully; and so must I! (Listens.)
I hear! '*The seventh rock behind the arch!*'

(He tries it; an explosion follows. The rocks all fall down, and are revealed as being in reality mere decorative papier-mache shells which *Masked Attendants* remove. Beside him stand *Mysta* and the *Mages*. The curtain-drop represents a six-story Babylonian Ziggurat or Babel-tower. From its summit a light flying Bridge reaches off into the clouds. To left or right are two great doors leading into the Tower; the left one shows in relief a lion, the right one a scarabæus. On the next higher platform stands a Bull chained to the wall by a heavy chain around his neck, he paws and snorts. The Mages are muffled in deep blue robes, and wear conical caps, Magus's showing the moon, and Maga's the sun. Between them stands an altar bearing a basket containing bread; a vessel containing sparkling ruby wine, and two crowns of papyrus reeds. Before it stands a stool, and on it the *Neophytes* are invited to place their feet, an Attendant removes their anklets, while says

Maga, Anklets, like ignorance, have shackled you;
   Henceforth released, the Truth will keep you free!

(On the block is placed a basin, and Maga washes the feet of Mystus, while Magus laves those of Mysta.)

Magi, Cleansed from sensation's dirt and suffering,
   Your feet support the vision of the Truth!
Magus, Too busy groping in the hopeless dark,
   Our urgent whispering you noticed not,
Maga, Till overwhelmed by pitiful despair,
   Silent, you caught the liberating Voice.
Magus, The sword of Pain shall crown you with the
                                    Truth!

(From beneath their robes the *Mages* produce two swords with which they lift the crowns to the *Neophytes*' brows.)

Neophytes, (refusing), Rather than take from sword,
     we 'ld lose the crowns!
 My crown is Truth, nor needs the sword's support!
Maga, Well said! For had you both accepted crowns
  From swords, *by* swords had you been robbed!

(With drawn swords *Attendants* spring upon the *Neophytes* who do not flinch. Then the swords are thrown before their feet, and the *Neophytes* step on them. Then *Maga* continues,)

  Which swords you now beneath your feet may
  Henceforth your only enemies are lies, [tread.
  Not the misguided souls who utter them!

Magus, Now since a crown not yet you may receive,
  Accept reminders of your destiny:
  These slender sprays that may adorn your hair,
  The immemorial sign of this Degree,
 Which shows who was received within these gates!

Maga, These branches further unto you denote
  The Tree of Life which flourishes on high
  Where neither night afflicts, nor tears can|grieve;
  For Truth itself is Temple, and gives light;
Whose priests, in snow-white robes, you now become.

(*Attendants* garb the *Neophytes* in white, and cause them to kneel down at the altar, and repeat the oath, line by line.)

Magus, I swear the Mysteries never to reveal;

Maga, I swear to use their knowledge for men's good;

Magus, I swear to abjure all violence by the sword,
  And e'er to fight hypocrisy and lies!

Maga, I swear to educate and cultivate,
  I swear to preach the Ministry of Truth!

(From the altar springs up fire which heats to a glowing point the irons with which the *Mages* brand the *Neophytes'* foreheads with a triangle.)

FIRST, WARRIOR

Mages, We seal you unto truth of every kind,
    To research, conscience, wisdom and to art;
    Warriors, rise as Centaur and Amazon!

Maga, No longer neophytes, but initiates,
    Your priesthood new you now must demonstrate
    By off'ring bread of immortality....

Magus, And dipping it into the glowing Drink
    Parturient with divinity, partake!

(They do so; *Attendants* blow trumpets, the blue robes drop from the *Mages,* who are revealed as fully armed.)

Magus, Now strengthened with the Bread of Life
    Of wrong use having grown incapable,   [eterne
    Restored to you all weapons now shall be,
    For now you face the real fight of life!

Maga, For be ye sure, that when you left brute force
    You did not enter on a life of ease;
While conscience slept, the world left you at peace;
Conscience awaked now claims from you your best,
    And you will need the Spirit's arms complete.

(From behind the altar *Attendants* bring the mentioned weapons with which the *Mages* deck the *Neophytes.*)

    Of Chastity the girdle, first your need;
    Second, the sandals of Decision firm;
    The sword of wise Discrimination;
    The bows and arrows of Prevailing Prayer,
    The breast-plate harp of full Sincerity,
    The star-crowned helmet of your Destiny!

    Endued with these, wrestling within yourselves,
    You shall subdue yon fiery snorting bull
    Guarding the Gate above us on the Tower
Thro' which you must find strength to force your way
  If you hold hope of progress through the spheres
    Of each successive planet, till you leave
    The summit of this Tower of Mysteries
    Along the swaying Bridge's razor path
    To follow on through all the further realms
    Of unseen planets undiscovered yet.

(From the Bull comes a terrible roar; the *Attendants* rattle their swords and shields, and drive the *Neophytes* through their respective gates. The *Mages* wave and cry 'Farewell!'

Maga, Your girdle, *Kosti*, stands for chastity
　　For this is needed in the search for Truth,
　　That you abstain from all entanglements
　　Of nature personal, and live henceforth
　　For principle, for reason, and for truth.
　　Of course, if you refuse to fight with men,
　　And turn the other cheek to him who smites,
　　You cannot hope to gain this world's success,
　　You will be poor; but then you will be free
　　To consecrate your heart to growth of soul.
　　The Gods will fight for you, if you will fight
　　Your lower natures, and the powers of air!

Magus, This is the pass-word of the First Degree:
　　As God is Truth, so all the Truth is God;
　　But Truth means *Progress unto Higher Facts*,
　　Who 'guards' it, kills it, out of laziness;
　　Needs not *defenders*, but needs *practisers*.

Maga, You sacred Centaur, you sweet Amazon,
　　This month, my children, you shall spend near us,
　　Watching the sun and constellated stars,
　　Learning the lessons of this special heav'n,
　　Gently preparing body, soul and mind
　　To break into the higher mystic Cave.

Magus, O Lord of Hosts, for knowledge we implore,
　　Quickness of tongue, and keen sagacity;
　　Give holiness of soul, and memory;
　　Grant understanding that shall ever grow,
　　The wisdom rooted in still fear of Thee.

Maga, With all good thoughts, with all good works,
With all good words, we come to thee, O God of Truth!
　　Whatever we believe to be pure and fair,
　　That will we think, and say, and do!
　　This course sincere, and without a useless parable
　　Is the best for the souls of men in both worlds!

✒ Questions to be Answered in Writing ✒

Not to be answered all at once, but each on the indicated day of the month, overlapping from 22nd to 22nd.

The ideal time to study this Degree alone is in February-March. If the whole series is to be taken, it is best to begin on April 22. But the first 22nd after you hear of these Degrees is the time Providence has set for *your* beginning; *anything* ranks delay.

DAY 22, Read the Degree aloud, and write it out in a fresh note-book large enough for the whole month. The object is not *curiosity-satisfaction* or *enjoyment*, but *experiences*, and a *growth*. Do all prayerfully.

Day 23, Memorize all the points of the Outline, and in a separate note-book for *Favorite Lines from All the Degrees* copy in your selections from this Degree.

Day 24, Write a prose essay on each Degree-part.

Day 25, Write a short essay on the *Manners of Deliverance*.

Day 26, Make a list of other *Dramas of the Search for Truth* of which you heard; make outlines.

Day 27, Describe the Mystery-Tower.

Day 28, Who were the Centaurs and Amazons, and what do they signify here?

Day 29, Relate and comment on the myth of the *Kinvat Bridge*, as narrow as a razor.

Day 30, Comment on the *Five Kinds of Truth* with which the Candidates were sealed.

Day 1, What Seven Kinds of Truth are prayed for?

Day 2, Read, from the *Apocrypha* the book of the *Wisdom of Solomon*, and memorize **5**.14-20.

Day 3, Read, from the *New Testament* Saint Paul's *Epistle to the Ephesians*, and memorize **6**.10-18.

Day 4, In what way could this Degree be improved? These your suggestions are asked, not for our sake, nor to ventilate your opinions, but to give you an opportunity to let the *Spirit* move you to utter *divine wisdom*, which we will gratefully welcome.

Practical Experiments to be Reported On.

Day 5-10, On six successive days take one each of the above-mentioned spiritual arms as your motto or key-note for the day, to solve whatever problems may arise. Note the results.

Day 11, Analyze which of these spiritual weapons is used by the people with whom you associate.

Day 12-14, In three problems that come up to you solve them by listening to the Inner Whisper; note the results.

Day 15, Make a list of the points of agreement between yourself and the most prominent organizations in your town.

Day 16, Try to get through one day without saying anything not true, kind or necessary.

Day 17, Try to fight with the untruths *in somebody* while retaining their personal friendship, attacking the problem impersonally. Note your success.

Day 18, During this day agree with everybody you meet, and note,

   a, How much you learn from even the most ignorant;

   b, How much you lose;

   c, How far you get from God, and how you can return to him, and how to keep in touch with him.

Day 19, Digest, re-read, summarize and evaluate all your results, and decide how much you have profited by the month's steady daily discipline; and even if you have achieved no more than to carry out in full this study-plan and experiments, you will have strengthened your will-power.

But the highest success for the Degree will consist of an unmistakable experience of interior initiation.

Day 20, 21, Gather everything together, return it to head-quarters without delay, asking the next Degree

SECOND DEGREE
The Bull
Achieving Continued Consciousness

The Mithraic Mysteries, Modernized.

Second Degree, the Bull

Major Points

1 **Symbol**, The Bull.
2 **Purpose**, Controlling of Sleep, and Achieving of Continued Consciousness.
3 **Scene**, Defending a Gate against a Wild Bull.
4 **Peculiarity**, In reality the Bull was chained, so that the only danger was fear. Against sleep the armor needed is not physical, but mental or spiritual. No physical means will insure sleep-control.
5 **Temptation**, To fall asleep.
6 **Oath**, Never to fall asleep without preliminary charging of sub-consciousness to awake at some predetermined time.
7 **Gift**, The Dagger of Mental Determination.

Minor Points

1 **Element**, Earth.
2 **Sign**, Aquarius or Ankle.
3 **Planet**, Mercury.
4 **Color**, Brown.
5 **Flower**, Lotus Bloom, which is amphibious.
6 **Jewel**, Bracelet.
7 **Token**, Lit candles, as light of heaven.

SECOND DEGREE

The Bull,—Achieving Continued Consciousness

(The back curtain representing the Mystery-tower having been lowered to the level of the second story of the platform, the scene represents the light blue Mercury floor surrounded by a parapet, leaving but a narrow balcony running across the front. In the centre is a huge double door showing a fierce bull in bas-relief. Benches stand on either hand of the door. It is a dark starry night. Twelve booms of a deep gong. The doors open forwards, revealing a central bull-shaped altar. By it stand *Magus* and *Maga* in light-blue robes and conical caps surmounted by Mercury, riding a sitting bull. Near them stand *Mystus & Mysta*.)

Magus, This is the night and hour when we shall see
    If you successfully your arms can wield!

(He claps; attendants bring two suits of armor which are laid on the outer benches, right and left.

Maga, Yourselves defending against ferocious bulls!

(*Maga* claps, and priests lead on two vicious bulls who paw and snort.)

Maga, If when the morning dawns you still are safe
    Nor have been tossed to death over the wall
    You shall be hailed as victors.

    (*Magus* from the balcony waves farewell to the *Neophytes.*)

Magus,   Now farewell!

    (As the doors gradually close the *Priests* sing,)

Priests, Hail, holy Bull, beneficent and strong,
    Who makest increase, and who grantest growth,
    Bestowing gifts on faithful souls unborn!
    As gathered waters in the Holy Sea,
    Rise upwards, go along the aerial way,

Descend to earth, — rise up and roll along!
And rise thou there, O Man, if thou be righteous too!

(The gates are closed, leaving the *Mystics* on their respective benches. When all, except the bellowing of the bulls, who seem to be rushing up against the doors, is silenced, *Mystus* chooses his arms.)

Mystus, Comrade, if you will help to buckle on
    My suit of armor, I will reciprocate!

(*Mysta* helps him; but when he holds out the armor for her, she gently but decisively refuses.)

Mysta, For your kind help, accept my heartfelt thanks
    But I prefer to fight with other arms.

Mystus, What other kind of arms could conquer bulls?

Mysta, You may rely on steel, but I on prayer.

Mystus, Women are cowards, for their prayers avail
    Only as men with swords their battles fight.
    You will be safe, because you trust to me
    Not only my own fight to make, but yours!

(He turns away in contempt, rejecting her expostulations, and picks up sword and shield.)

Mystus, You can afford to spin your theories
    Because I fight two bulls instead of one!

(He strides up and down; when under the impact of the bulls the doors shake again, he throws himself against them with his whole weight. When their fury abates, he returns to his seat, and being weary falls asleep. There is heard the following)

Chorus, She stands, the River Anahita, the
    Water of Life, clad in a golden cope.
  She asks, Whom shall I hold!? Who holds to me?
O Water firmamental that feedest the Roots of the Tree
                             of Life,
O lustral Water that sparklest in the sacramental Cup,
O spiritual torrent that bearest the seeds of living things

SECOND, *the* BULL,

That enduest men with hair, and the women with tend-
er grace,
O dew from Heaven that rousest the flowers to fragrance
O silver drops that sparkle in rainbow hues when the
moonshine thrills in them,
You do we worship, cleave to, and adore!

(Suddenly the bulls bellow more furiously than ever, rattling the doors as if to burst them. *Mysta* wakes *Mystus*, who jumps up angrily, throws himself against the doors, and makes a barricade with *Mysta's* unused armor.)

Mystus, That was a violent start from peaceful sleep!
    I dreamed that I was awake! How pitiful
    To fall asleep, for me who often have
    Watched through a night in studies, or in field!
    I feel oppressed by bands around my head!

Mysta, I also almost slept; but from within
    A crystal bell aroused me, even thrice,—
    So that I knew that God approves my prayers.

(The bulls bellow and shake the doors more than ever; but a gong strikes six times, the doors slide back, revealing the *Mages* standing on either side of an altar, surrounded by priests, all vested in salmon colored robes, who lead out the bulls that are plainly seen to be securely fastened by ropes to their nose-rings, while the *Priests* are singing the)

Chorus, Full of good thoughts, good words and good
deeds,
O Seven Spirits of God, to You I sacrifice my prayers,
Prepared to yield my life for the good of my soul!

(At an inviting gesture of the *Mages*, the *Mystics* attempt to enter the portal, but are hindered by a black-masked *Figure* who wears many bracelets and makes many gestures, brandishing a sword, crying,)

Figure, You may not enter till you pay the price:
    Who gives no bracelet shall not enter here!

SECOND, *the* BULL

(**The amazed** M*ystics* look at their bracelets, which **they had** forgotten; M*ystа* gracefully removes hers, and places them on the point of the outstretched sword, along which it glides to the *Figure's* wrist. M*ystus*, however, angrily throws his bracelets at the *Figure*, who refuses to pick them up, attacks M*ystus*, and compels him to get on his knees and pick them up, and place them on the sword's point; whereupon he disappears. In front of the altar there is placed a small stand bearing a golden ewer, basin and towels.)

Maga, Halt till you understand the fee you paid.
    As if by manacles around your wrists,
  By bracelets symboled, Sleep has kept you bound.
    But conquering that bull within yourselves,
    For mental gyves I now shall substitute
    The outward sign of self-control;
    And as I lave your hands with water cool,
    Sleep's enemy, rousing from drowsiness,
    Intoxicating dreams evaporate.

      (Pointing to their purified hands, says)

Magus, I greet you unto waking sanity!
    Have you forgotten what last month you learned?
    We never wrestle with mere flesh and blood,
    But with the forces in our moral world.
    Who iron arms assumed, was tempted most.
The bulls were chained; the doors, though movable,
    Could never have been burst, for they slide in.
    This initiation, if consisting of
    A struggle physical with genuine bulls,
    For women and for children were impossible,
Though they, as much as men, shall enter heaven.
    You needed spiritual armor here!

(Pointing to the Tauromachic sculptures of men fighting with uprearing bulls, plunging daggers in their sides, says)

Maga, Nor either is this dagger physical;

SECOND, *the* BULL

It is the praying mind's incisiveness.

(The *Mages* hand to each *Mystic* a dagger.)

Plunging this dagger in the altar's side,
Kneel, and swear oath that shall your souls promote!

(As the Mystics thus use their daggers, blood flows from the altar's wound. They kneel and repeat,)

Oath, I swear to minimize and clarify
    And sanctify my sleep by tireless prayer;
I will not sleep without clear hours to wake.
I swear to keep my sleep within control;
I swear to keep my consciousness therethrough,
So that I may preserve it also when
I shall elect to leave my body's inn!

(*Magus* places a white lotus leaf wreath around each *Mystics'* neck: and they are attired in light blue robes.]

Magus, We hail you Bulls celestial, both of you,
    You ankle-hinges of humanity!
For such control of sleep permits a soul
To run along the paths of Destiny.
The amphibious lotus-blooms clearly denote
That you henceforth are citizens of both:
Of earth, and the Unseen surrounding this,
Living below as pupils for above.

[Clouds of smoke begin to rise from the two braziers before the two doors in the back, to right and left of the altar; the left one is the silver *Dream Door of Horn,* the right one is the golden *Vision Door of Ivory.*]

Maga, Cease, O MAGUS; I choke, I faint, I fail!
Magus, Unconsciously I have evoked the Shades!
First Priest, A mist beclouds my mental faculties!
Second Priest, Dizzy, the world is whirling to an end!

[In sleep they all sink down to the ground. Coming through the left Door of Dreams, blowing out the candles on the altar, says a]

SECOND, the BULL

Fiend, I give the dreams fantastic and confused
   That agitate the souls whose sleep is wild,—
   Devoid of limit, purpose, quality.
   Nightmares of shame and crime I bring.
   But why find fault with me, who only go
   Where sleepers open unto me the door
   By lack of prayer, and mean unconsciousness?
   Come, DEMONS, here is opportunity!

(Enter the *Demons* who dance fantastically among the sleeping forms, specially insulting the *Mystics*. Some, resembling beautiful women, throw themselves on the sleepers; others, resembling savage beasts, pour opiates into the sleepers' mouths and ears. Suddenly are heard the soft beginnings of a gradually increasing sacred *Chorus*, during which the *Demons* increasingly manifest first anxiety, later turning to terror; they finally remain transfixed in picturesque attitudes of terror.)

Chorus, O upright Soul, for wisdom seek of Me,
   Who am the most pleased in listening to the prayer
                              for light.

   What is it that makes the unseen power of Death
                              increase?

   He who sleeps unconsciously all through the night
   Without sacrament, without hymns, without teach-
                              ings and prayers.

   Who sets the world in motion to obedience and law?
   The unseen spiritual Cocks, the Drums of the world
   Who flit through the night, to wake from sleep:
   'Arise, O Men, recite the prayers that smite down
                              the Demons!'

   While the yellow, long-handed, lurid Demon lulls,
   'Sleep on, O Man, the time for prayer has not yet come!'
   But the spiritual Cocks lift up their voice against the
                              mighty dawn:

   'In each part of the night descends the Spiritual Fire.
   Up, House-holder, with washed hands, bring me
      pure deeds, that I may burn up bright!

SECOND, *the BULL,*

Thus the Spiritual Cocks lift up their voices before the mighty Dawn.
Whichever of you men first rises shall first enter Paradise
And he who saves his vitality from the demons of the last shades of night,
He shall never be questioned at all,
He shall directly enter Paradise!

(The *Good Genius* enters through the right hand *Door of Visions,* followed by the other *Geniuses* who carry lighted tapers. The *Demons* cry out for mercy, as if in pain, especially the *Fiend*. They group themselves around their door, as if loth to leave Among and around the prostrate forms the *Good Genius* leads the procession of *Geniuses* who deposit their candle-sticks on the altar in a semi-circle, whose centre is forwards.)

[Carrying a rosary, says the]
First Genius, The light of prayer drives out unworthy shades
And summons helpers; vanish, Indolence!
(With a cry, the *First Demon* disappears.)

(Holding a cock, says the)
Second Genius, LIMIT, the Gnostic deity, is wise
And intellectualizes; flee, Excess! [He flees.]

[Holding a fly-wheel, says the]
Third Genius, Habit is banister of upward stairs;
So vanish, Irresponsibility! [He flees.]

[Carrying a compass, says the]
Fourth Genius, Guidance can clear the dreams of the perplexed;
Chiefly when waking up. So perish, Doubt! [He flees.]

[Carrying a bell, says the)
Fifth Genius, Warnings will save from the approach of ill;
Only for drones are oracles; so perish, Fate! [He flees

(*The five Geniuses are grouped in a semi-circle around the altar. From within this, in the centre, appears Immortality, a maiden, in a white robe and golden crown, bearing a palm, with wings on her feet, like Mercury.*)

Immortality, Life is a school of Immortality;
    I am not *creed,* as theologians say;
    I am not *philosophical view* of God.

    Attainment is not merely mystic truth,
    No sudden knowledge, momentary glimpse,
    No death-bed gift of generous Deity;
    Free is the truth of facts, but not results,
    Which follow daily, weekly, yearly growth.

    Thus shall you cull each morn a spirit-rose
    Rooted in you unto immortal life.
    If by the aid of these Good Geniuses
    Your sleep becomes development and growth
Then, while you rest, your soul may visit heaven,
Bringing you news and cheer and strength to rise.

    Then when you shall, as all have ever done,
    Relinquish all your body to the dust,
    The change will be no more than daily trick,
    And with full consciousness you may proceed.

    This is the meaning of your immortality,
    Which he may gain who earns it in this life;
    If not, in spite of all theologies
    And rites and promises, you fall asleep.

(*Immortality disappears, and during this speech the Geniuses, one by one, have retired through the Vision-door. The Mages and Attendants have sat up, listening; they rise, wave farewell, and cry,*)

All, Farewell, O mystic Conquerors of sleep;
    Avoid temptation, watching unto prayer!

Questions to be Answered in Writing 🖎 2

Not to be answered all at once, but each on the indicated
day of the month, overlapping from 22nd to 22nd.

The ideal time to study this Degree alone is in Jan'ry-February
If the whole series is to be taken, it is best to begin on May 22

But the first 22nd after you hear of these Degrees is the time
Providence has set for *your* beginning; *anything* ranks delay.

DAY 22, Read and copy the Degree, and memorize the duly recorded favorite selections therefrom.

Day 23, Explain why the Bull well represents the physical nature of sleep.

Day 24, What does the *River Anahita* represent?

Day 25, What does the bracelet represent?

Day 26, Illustrate the oath's significance and implications.

Day 27, Explain the message and significance of the *Fiend*.

Day 28, Memorize and write out your interpretation of the message of the *First Good Genius*.

Day 29, Memorize the message of the *Second Good Genius*, and write out your interpretation.

Day 30, Memorize the message of the *Third Good Genius*, and write out your interpretation.

Day 1, Memorize the message of the *Fourth Good Genius*, and write out your interpretation.

Day 2, Memorize the message of the *Fifth Good Genius*, and write out your interpretation.

Day 3, Memorize the message of the *Sixth Good Genius*, and write out your interpretation.

Day 4, Memorize the message of *Immortality*, and write out your interpretation thereof.

❧ Practical Experiments for Reports. ❧ 2

Day 5, Observe and note the *Different Kinds of Sleep-Feelings* in fore-noon, afternoon.

Day 6, Note the *dryness* of the sleep after theatre.

Day 7, On going to sleep let the last thought be a charge to the sub-consciousness to wake up at a specified time, success being possible to all.

Day 8, During waking hours practise laying down the body passively, and picking it up at some specified time, *e.g.*, 1, 2, or 3 minutes. This is to develop mental control over the body.

Day 9, Lie down first; then decide to raise the body when you have counted regularly 10, 15 or 25.

Day 10, Do the same, varying the rate of counting, at fancy, as a sort of bravado challenge to the body to make it realize its subservience to the mind.

Days 11-14, Take sufficient rest beforehand to be able to stay awake *entirely* from 12 pm to 8 am. Observe
1, The *First Vitality Period*, 3-5 am.
2, About 6 am the momentary *noddings*.
3, About 7 am the *Second Vitality Period*.
4, Note its flashes of dream-vision.
5, Notice the subsequent *Fragrant Happiness*.

Days 15-17, Observe that when you are sincerely trying to keep awake all night, or even only at the vitality-times, you will be waked, (three times and no more,) from within, by the ringing of a bell, a knock, a slap, a dream, — but never twice the same way, — proving there are *Helpers*, and that the object is worth while.

Day 18, Observe the contrariness of circumstances of falling asleep or waking up just too late, as soon as you have formed some plan of a regular prayer hour, at night or in the morning, proving there are *Hinderers*.

Day 19, First during rest, then during sleep learn to achieve *Continued Consciousness*.

THIRD DEGREE

The Lion

Preservation of Health

The Mithraic Mysteries, Modernized.

Third Degree, the Lion

Major Points

1 **Symbol**, The Lion.
2 **Purpose**, Achievement and Preservation of Health.
3 **Scene**, The Temple Garden, with its shrubs and flowers.
4 **Peculiarity**, There are dangers even among flowers.
5 **Temptation**, To help others in disobedience to rules of conscience.
6 **Oath**, To keep and improve health.
7 **Gift**, The Tri-faced Cylinder.

Minor Points

1 **Element**, Earth.
2 **Sign**, Capricorn or Knees.
3 **Planet**, Venus.
4 **Color**, Red.
5 **Flower**, Pink Nelumbo Lotus.
6 **Jewel**, Girdle.
7 **Token**, Sprinkling.

THIRD DEGREE

The Lion, — Preservation of Health

(The Mystery-tower drop being lowered, the scene represents the third or Venus-story, colored pink. A railing across the front of the stage, with centre steps leading down to the ground floor. There are two seats, one on each side of the central door, on which is sculptured a lion, and from within is heard a lion's roar. From behind the scenes is heard the following)

Chorus, I proclaim the easiest path to the Mountain of Serene Abode
    Of all the seven-fold Archangelic Host,
    Leading first through the Good Thought Paradise,
    The path whose second station is the Good Word Paradise,
    The path whose third station is the Good Deed Paradise;
    And thence those bright and wise and holy ways
    Lead up unto serene abodes of endless lights
    Where holiness shall be enthroned on perfect health.
Which then are words that may increase this health?

(A *Priest* steps to the front, raises a silver trumpet, and blows until up through the aisles of the auditorium come *Mystus* and *Mysta*, who seat themselves on their respective benches. They seem dusty, tired and sick.)

Mystus, I do not understand this sudden call.
    Only last night we passed the Second Degree;
    So I supposed that we might rest a month
    Before a call unto some further step.

Mysta, And so thought I, although but yestermorn
    We were enjoined unsleeping watchfulness.
    Courage! Unto the brave all news is good;
    Of all they make an opportunity;
    Out of misfortune wise ones progress make,
    Unto the evil, fortune is a curse;
    Short shrift below means longer bliss above.

Mystus, Not cowardly is my perplexity.
    I longed for time just to improve myself,
    In habit's crucible to sublimate
    My vows into a virtuous character.
    The bleeding of my wound is staunched;
    But struggling with wild beasts is not for me.
    MYSTA, I will not hinder you; — I stay.

(*Magus* appears from the left, and from the right *Maga*.)

Magus, It is not we who drive; return who can!
    Have you observed that your retreat is blocked?

(Armed soldiers guard all exits; consternation; from within, roars of the lion.)

Mystus, So we are trapped?

Maga,   By your own fear of death
    Which if you ask for, they will not refuse,
    Servants of fate that hounds the recreant!
    Rather, rejoice promotion is advanced;
    It is a privilege, a special grace
    To leonine achievement to progress.
    Who with ideals taurine is content,
    May stay behind; which one elects to stay?

Mysta, We will proceed, but we are sick.

Magus,   How so?
    You were enjoined to stay within the Tower;
    What evil influence could reach you there?

Mystus, (shamefacedly,) Strolling last night amidst the garden's peace,
    I met a maid engaged in gathering flowers.
    Struggling to pluck a rose, she sought for help
    Which giving I so deeply stung myself
    That more than even then I suffer now.
    (He unwraps the bandage; the swollen hand bleeds.)
    The bush must have been poisoned, for the girl
    Suddenly grew hideous, and disappeared,
    Her mocking cries reechoing afar.

Maga, My son, that girl was demon SAENI,
    'Brood of the Snake,' who multiplies all ills.
    Bandage again your hand, and wait until
    MYSTA confesses how she too was hurt.

Mysta, I met a youth who seemed transfixed by pain.
    As if athirst, he moaned; I crushed some fruit
    Into a cooling draught. Refreshed he rose,
    And gratefully insisted I partake
    Thereof myself; but as I drank of it,
    I burned with fever, while he fled with jeers.

Magus, Daughter, the demon BASI was that youth,
    Surnamed the '*Barker;*' piteously he pleads,
    Yet those who fail in judgment he infects.
    So neither one escaped the demons' trap!

Mcga, Can both of you be ready for this morn?

Mystus, Ready at heart, I faint. Oh heal me first!

Magus, That neither one may fail shall be my prayer!
    (To the *Mystics'* consternation, the *Mages* pass out.)

Mysta, Not yet I hear, but feel the knock of Fate!

Mystus, Unto the lions I shall throw myself!
    (The lions' roar is heard through the gates.)

Mysta, If God can save, he still can save us now!

Mystus, Abandoned, we shall have to save ourselves!

Mysta, So let us heal each others' suffering:
>Your hand heroic treatment now demands.
>>(She takes *Mystus's* knife, pulls out the thorn.)

Here prayer is vain, — we must invoke the knife,
>As only Judgment sin entrenched can cure.
>But this removed, now other healing helps.
>>(She breaks off a twig and gives it to him to chew.)
>
>Some cooling herbs; later, hygienic rest.
>Are you relieved?

Mystus,   If you will rub the arms
>Close to the shoulders, it will ease the pain.
>My head still aches, however!

Mysta,   I will hold
>Your forehead.

Mystus,   Now the pain has passed away.
>>(*Mysta* falls in a swoon.)
>
>Selfishly I had forgotten you!
>>(He loosens her dress, and chafes her hands.)
>
>The power of the Word! Look well at me!

(Stares at her; her eyes open; he commands, *Mysta, Mysta!*)

Mysta, I hear you, and obey!

Mystus, The whole of your mischance you have forgot
>Sleep now; then wake in perfect health, and rise!

(She soon awakes, and rises cheerfully. While the *Neophytes* recover themselves entirely there is heard a]

Chorus, Willingly will we increase best righteousness;
>But with what words may we increase good health?
>For one will heal with the knife in surgery,

And smite to death the germinating brood of the Snake.
>For one will heal with the herbs in medicine,

And smite to death the wildering fevers that parch.

THIRD, *the* LION

    For one will heal with the methods of hygiene,
And smite to death the disastrous habits of ill.
    Another one will heal by quickening the nerves
And smite to death the palsy of bewildered muscles.
    Another one will heal with magic of the word
And smite to death the evil eye of sin.
    For one will heal by cleansing antiseptical,
And smite to death the swarming brood of germs.
    But best he heals who uses righteousness in deed,
Who smites to death the sins of wicked men,
Who lives up to his standards in the best of lights,
He best shall free the Faithful from the handicap of pain
So he be unmolested in his sacrifice of prayer and praise.

(Suddenly a flourish of trumpets; the portals open, revealing the two altars, at which stand the *Mages*. In front crouches a lion chained down to the floor by each foot; he roars only when beaten by an *Attendant*.]

Magus, This is the lion that you so much feared,
    You foolish neophytes. — Have him removed!

Maga, But he has served you, if the fear of him
Nerved you to make yourselves achieve good health
    To conquer in yourselves the lions of
    Disease and pain and grief and evil thoughts.

(As *Magus* turns back, the *Initiates* move to approach the two altars; but they are roughly jostled back by a black-faced Porter wearing anklets, bracelets and a jeweled girdle, brandishing a sword, and shouting,)

Porter, None enters here who does not pay the price;
    Who gives no jeweled girdle stays without!

(The *Mystics* unclasp their girdles and hand them to the *Porter* who with a shout of triumph disappears through the floor. Behind *Maga* at the altar stand the *Attendants* holding two lion's skins which are later draped around the *Mystics*.)

THIRD, *the LION*

Maga, Anklets of ignorance first you doffed,
    Bracelets of deep unconsciousness next;
    Remains the Venus-girdle of disease
  Hanging around your waist, which you must doff
    So gradual lustration purify.

(She sprinkles their waists with water from the altar, whereafter the *Attendants* bind around their waists wreaths of pink lotus, or *pyx-nelumbo* flowers.)

Magus, These lotus-flowers, symbolic of good health,
    Have roots in mud, but rise into a bush
    With grains for food, and calyces for cups.
  Its leaves make vessels, and its roots make bread,
    Useful and fragrant, also beautiful.

(On their shoulders *Attendants* drape the lion-skin mantles; they kneel at the altar and raise their hands for the oath,)

Oath, I swear to fight the lion of disease,
    I swear to heal all suffering I meet,
    I swear to be example of good health!

Magus, As tokens of initiation
    Accept these tri-faced cylinders, engraved
    With Horse and Bull and Lion, — three Degrees.
    Even within your coffins, keep them near
    As testifying you have qualified
    As hygienists through spiritual means,
    Intoning praises of the healing Gods!

Maga, Lions alone dare see the sacrament;
    Attendants, go, and drive all others out!

(*Attendants* go around and demand to see every person's cylinder, whereupon they lock the doors to right and left and return,)

Attendants, We have examined all, and all is well!

Chorus, O praise ye the Archangel of health and com-
                            pleteness,

THIRD, *the LION*

Praise ye the Master of prosperity and wholesomeness
For the help, enjoyments, comforts and pleasures of health.

The man who is most faithful shall be the healthiest too
He shall part from the way of evil by cleansing himself,
By keeping mysterious the threefold prayer of son and brother and pupil;
Then, devoted to law, holy and brave, he shall still all his pains.

He asked the Archangel of Health for remedies
To heal the suffering, and preserve the young;
Plants was he given, grown round the Tree of Life
That grows by the Cloud-Sea on the Holy Mount.
These are the prayers by which he drives it away:
Avaunt, O Sickness, Pain, Fever, Disease and Death!
The desirable reward is that won by compliance with the Holy Law,
That blessed boon for holiness vouchsafed by the Lord!

Magus, O Providence and Destiny, be gracious to me while I am pronouncing these Thy first traditional Mysteries; for in the silence of meditation I was only-begotten of the Immortal by the secrets of this our rite being revealed to me at command of the First-born, by his archangel the planet Venus, so that I might ascend into his awful Heavens, where I might behold all things face to face!

Maga, First Origin of my origin, Fire which, for my progression, was given to me by God that I might be initiated, and that the Holy Spirit might breathe in me, that I might behold the Abyss, and the horror-striking flood of Sunrise: and that the bivifying circumambient Ether, the Master of the Fire-crowns, might listen to me, a Mortal born with the up-springing golden sheen of flame of the Immortal Lamp!

Both Mages, STAND STILL, O PERISHABLE HUMAN NATURE, AND IMMEDIATELY LET ME LOOSE AFTER THIS PITILESS PRESSING NEED, FOR I ALSO AM THE SON OF GOD!

Magus, Arouse, O Souls under the altar!

Maga, Arise, great Healer of the universe!

(Suddenly the front of the altar opens in two doors, and from it emerge flames.)

Magus, All altar-lights are symbols of this Fire
    Yet unextinguished from eternity.
    He is the Healer of the universe
    Who kills all low, unworthy forms of life,
    And thereby helps the higher forms of life.
    Listen unto the Altar-souls complain!

First Voice, I am the refuse of the sacrifice!

Second Voice, I am the germs contagious of disease!

Third Voice, I am the useless members dying out!

Fourth Voice, I am the offal breeding lice and flies!

Fire, I am the Fire that is the Friend of God,
    Destroying evermore low forms of good
    So higher forms find ample room to thrive.
    In sanctuary of every human heart
    I scarify low impulse and desire
    That high ideals may be realized;
So he who 'ld hold his health must work and cleanse.
    There is an inward cause for every pain,
    Some old ideal buried and forgot.
    While living contrary to soul's desire,
    O'er flesh the soul cannot preponderate
    So as to keep its functions flowing smooth;
    Nor, scorned, can master the rebellious flesh.
    So, healers, catch my flame ere I retire!

THIRD, *the* LION

(The *Mystics* light torches at the *Fire* which, amidst the moaning of the *Lower Forms of Life*, dies down as the Altar-doors close.)

Magus, So now, dear MYSTICS, you will understand
    Why crucifixion is the law of health;
    Why sacrifice of self is virtue's root;
    Why those who let the fire of effort die
    Collapse into decay gelatinous.

Maga, So earth cannot be heaven until some fire
    Burn up the bundles of the prickly weeds;
    Why hell must cause to perish every wrong;
    Why you, Apostles of Hygiene and Light
    Will have to meet with opposition sore.

Magus, Farewell, ye LIONS, look unto your fires!

Maga, At night, by prayers from stars renew their glow!

Closing Chorus, Who art thou? asks radiant HUMILITY
    Why prayest thou to me?
I will give thee glory of body, and cheerfulness of soul;
    Fragrance and graciousness, and alluring health.
    This is the sacrifice best loved by Immortals:
Wisdom of tongue, and holy prayer and perfect words,
Strong and welfare-giving, healing, powerful of mind.
Such is GOOD HEALTH, sister of the Archangelic Host,
But daughter of sweet HUMILITY, mother of God,
Endowing all the Helpers of the Restoration of the world
With enlivening intelligence, to promote eternal life!

Questions to be Answered in Writing 🏳 3

Not to be answered all at once, but each on the indicated day of the month, overlapping from 22nd to 22nd.

The ideal time to study this Degree alone is in December-Jan'ry
If the whole series is to be taken, it is best to begin on June 22
But the first 22nd after you hear of these Degrees is the time Providence has set for *your* beginning; *anything* ranks delay.

Day 22, Read and copy the Degree, and memorize your favorite selections therefrom, and record them.

Day 23, Explain the mutual and progressive relation between the Search for Truth, the Control of Sleep, and the Achievement of Health.

Day 24, What is represented by the girdle?

Day 25, Tell all the uses of the *Nelumbo Lotus*, and its significance for the Achievement of Health.

Day 26, What is the best secret of Good Health.

Day 27, Explain the significance of the *First Demon*.

Day 28, Explain the significance of the *Second Demon*.

Day 29, Memorize and reproduce the *Mithraic Prayers*

Day 30, Explain *Crucifixion* as the First Law of Health

Day 1, What is the sacrifice best loved by the Immortals?

Day 2, Memorize and reproduce in writing the Oath.

Day 3, Explain the Significance of the *Four Souls Under the Altar*.

Day 4, Explain the significance of Fire as Purifier; and of the Parsee Fire-worship.

Day 5, Study and abstract the *Song of Healing*, or other outline of the various methods of healing.

Practical Experiments to be Reported ❧ 3

The object of this month's experiments is to gain some practical knowledge of the various methods of healing; but many readers will be circumstanced so as to find it extremely difficult to do, anything else than to borrow books from libraries, buy books, or visit hospitals, practicioners or exponents of each system. As every person has some weakest spot in in his body, the cure of this should be undertaken.

The special result is to be some expertry in each, and clear realization of *each system's special fields of maximum and minimum efficiency.* But everybody *must know something practical about each.*

Day 6, Surgery, especially minor first-aid operations such as treating a small cut, bandaging, removing cinders from the eye, extracting a splinter from the hand. Here belongs dentistry. See an operation.

Day 7, Drugs, allopathy. Go out and pick some remedial herb, to make a poultice or infusion.

Day 8, Homœopathy (misnamed,) the same drugs as above, only in quantities so infinitesimal as to allow nature to form anti-bodies, for immunity.

Day 9, Hygiene, antisepsis, nature cures, baths.

Day 10, Diet, and the value & combination of foods.

Day 11, Cooking; everybody should be able to prepare a few of the chief necessities of life.

Day 12, Massage or scientific caressing of muscles.

Day 13, Osteopathy, scientific treatment of nerves.

Day 14, Chiropractic, treatment of nerve-centres.

Day 15, Electricity, violet rays, X-rays.

Day 16, Magnetism, color treatments, solar baths.

Day 17, Hypnotism, suggestion, auto-suggestion.

Day 18, Stoicism, metaphysics: right philosophy.

Day 19, Religion, avoiding fetishes, quacks & idols.

FOURTH DEGREE

The Vulture

Comparative Religion

The Mithraic Mysteries, Modernized.

Fourth Degree, the Vulture

Major Points

1 **Symbol**, The Vulture.
2 **Purpose**, The Truest Religion.
3 **Scene**, The Mystery-tower. Statues of various divinities contain doves, desire for which induces the Vulture to destroy all the statues.
4 **Peculiarity**, The Initiates cannot enter until they call on God.
5 **Temptation**, To lose faith in God because of the destruction of some lower image.
6 **Oath**, Not to destroy another man's faith needlessly.
7 **Gift**, A rosary.
8 **Soul-part**, Emotions and Mind.

Minor Points

1 **Element**, Water.
2 **Sign**, Saggittarius or Thighs.
3 **Planet**, Mars.
4 **Color**, Pink.
5 **Flower**, Colocasia Blooms.
6 **Jewel**, Breast-pin.
7 **Sign-parts**, Lepus, Auriga, Columba.

FOURTH DEGREE

The Vulture, — Against Sectarianism

(The Mystery-tower drop is let down one more story. A narrow balcony, on which are bas-reliefs of Mars, and an arrow. The color is purple, *Attendants* lead on the *Mystics* clad in purple in response to the blowing of a silver trumpet by a priest. *Mystus* is led to a small side door, and the *Attendant* knocks.)

Magus, [from within,] Who knocks?

Mystus, MYSTUS would here admittance find.

Magus, What price have you to pay?

Mystus, My breast-pin's gold. [Pushes it in].

Magus, What seek you here?

Mystus, Truest religion's form.

Magus, Why should I aid you in this further search?

Mystus, If you refuse, the God of Truth will help.
    Shining Apollo, open me the door!

(Thunder-peals. In two vases, at each side of the door, is burning incense. *Attendants* poke the flames, till they seem to bar the door, which opens. *Mystus* seeks to enter, but hesitates at the fire. He cries,)

Mystus, Apollo, help!

Magus,   And should Apollo help
    Merely because his name was on your lips?

Mystus, My dream was to become a perfect sage,
    A gentleman with heart magnanimous
    Living along best moderation's path,

FOURTH, *the* VULTURE

I would unravel true philosophy,
And so I claim admittance from its God!

(*Attendants* turn the vases outwards, permitting him to enter. Again the gong sounds, and *Mysta* is led to the small right hand door, at which she knocks. Then is heard the voice of)

Maga, Who knocks?

Mysta, Mysta would here admittance find.

Maga, What price have you to pay?

Mysta, My breast-pin's gold (pushing it in.)

Maga, Why would you come?

Mysta, On grounds of holiness.

Maga, Strong are your grounds but stronger is the lock

Mysta, But strongest is the help of Hand divine.

Maga, Help shall you have, if you can demonstrate
    You understand and merit what you seek.
    Why did you come?

Mysta, It was my mother's wish.

Maga, Good reason, for the mothers' sacred name
    Will open any door in earth or heaven.
    But what the reason of your mother's wish?

Mysta, To God's most holy Will I had resigned
    The vibrant voices of tumultuous sense;
    I would conform myself unto the Law,
    And unto Circumstance adapt my steps.
    Devotion, humble simple-mindedness,
    Is all I know; is that enough to save?

Maga,   Not quite.

Mysta, Then am I lost; — O Ishtar, save!

(She swoons, but is saved from falling by an *Attendant;* the vases are turned away. *Maga* steps out and embraces her.]

Maga, In your despair you have redeemed yourself;

FOURTH, *the* VULTURE

    With tears I waited till you called on Heaven:
    Not until then was entrance possible.
    Oh what a grief unto immortal hearts
    Are humans who mistake morality
    For spiritual progress unto heaven,
      In which alone the Gods may dare assist.
    Dear, you are saved, although so very late!

(The large doors open, revealing a central altar. Around it in a semi-circle are ranged statues. Beginning with the left they represent Apollo, the Trimourti, Thor, Jupiter, the Druid Hesus, Isis and Ishtar. The *Mystics* are seated on either extremity, near the divinity each called on. At a sign from *Magus* they are blind-folded and made to kneel at the altar.)

Magus, Children, you are attired in flowing robes
    Which show that you rely on Truth, not Force.
    Their purple color is the hue of Mars,
    The militant divine iconoclast.
    You sacrificed your breast-pin to denote
    That you resigned religious amulets.
    Blind-folded you are still, to typify
    The earthly state of you, who shall see God.
    So, ere the bandage be removed, kneel down
    And swear not to divulge the mystery!

Mystics, What now shall be revealed, we vow to keep
    Inviolate until our dying day!

(On being led back to their seats, the bandages are removed from the *Mystics* who then for the first time behold, and seem impressed by the six plaster statues, from each of which proceeds the faint cooing of a dove. On the altar stands a vulture, chained. On hearing the cooing, the vulture grows restless, straining to destroy the statues, so as to get at the doves they contain. At a nod from *Maga* its fetters are lengthened so as to enable the vulture to peck the statues to pieces. From each escapes a white dove which, as its statue is demolished, escapes to the foot of the altar. In turn cry the)

FOURTH, *the* VULTURE

Attendants, Apollo dies, but knowledge shall survive!
    Thor dies, but law eternal shall survive!
    Trimourti perishes, but love remains!
    Isis dies, immortality persists!
    Druid oaks fall, but Nature flourishes!
    E'en Jupiter shall fail, but wealth remains!
    Ishtar shall fail, devotion shall endure!

(As the vulture rages at loss of its prey, flames ascend from each statue's ruins; but its chains are again shortened, so that it is again restricted to the pedestal on which it stands, and which sinks out of sight through the floor. In the meanwhile *Attendants* drape on the *Mystics* robes of vulture feathers, with vulture-masks over their faces.)

Maga, O sacred Vultures, you now understand
    That like reformers you must hew down gods,
    And burn their pieces with consuming fire.
    You will not harm divinity within,
    For on the altar now the doves are safe.
    The fire is sacred, for it burned to ash
    All tribal, racial, language-born mistakes.
    It melts hard metals, so they take new shape,
    As spiritual ardor moulds your souls,
    You spirit-vulturous iconoclasts!

    As fire guards health, it keeps religion pure.
    The doves were knowledge and beneficence,
    Conformity to law and sovereignty,
    Devotion, health and immortality.

    With all these principles divested of
    Old racial, tribal animosities,
    No longer will each fight against the next,
    For all will be revealed completing parts
    Of the organic world-divinity.

FOURTH, *the* VULTURE

Magus, Such vulturous service to humankind
 Gave Amen-hotep, Moses, Mahomet,
 Buddha; — but mostly our Zoroaster,
 Though in his language his divinities
 Meant only Knowledge and Beneficence,
 Conformity to Law and Sovereignty,
 And Piety, Health and Immortality.

 When his Avestan language was forgot,
 These words Ahura-Mazda, Vohu-Mano,
 Kshathra-Vairyia, Spenta Armaiti,
 And Haurvatat, and last Ameretat,
 Remained as fetishes; wherefore again
 The same iconoclasm was in demand.

 You sacred Vultures must therefore again
 Fly up and break these statues into dust,
 Since God is Knowledge, Word, Conformity,
 Wealth, Piety, Health, Immortality.

 Then too, Knowledge is God, and all the rest;
 And as these principles abide in you,
 So are you gods, and have become divine.

Maga, Call them the Spirits of True Knowledge,
 Of Understanding and True Holiness,
 Of Might, of Piety, of Health eterne,
 As did Isaiah, in another land.
 The Seven Spirits of the Throne of God,
 The Seven Archangels of the Heavenly Host,
 By Them inspired may your spirits shine!
 The Archangels, the bright ones, whose looks
     perform their wish;
 Who all seven were of one thought, one speech,
     one deed,
 Who have one same Father and Commander,
 Who see each other's soul thinking, speaking
     and acting well,

Whose ways are shining as they descend to men's prayers,
Who are makers and governors, shapers and overseers,
Keepers and preservers of the creation of the Lord
It is They and their agreement that shall restore the world,
That never henceforth shall grow old or die,
Master of its wish when the dead shall rise,
When life and immortality shall come,
And the world be restored at its wish.

Mystus, But lo, the seven doves have joined upon
    The self-same altar, . .

Mysta,   And the self-same fires
    Extinguished now, a single beam shoots up
    On the central altar, midst the seven doves.
    Within that beam, oh could we see the Truth!

Magus, We can evoke that vision by a chant,
    By rosary of holy names of God.

(*Attendants* distribute rosaries, and give directions how to use them.)

Magus, God is so various that a hundred names
    Would not suffice his self to represent;
    So while the Seven Archangels can express
    The chief foundations of His holiness,
    Himself appears in different form each day,
    Each morn responding to a diff'rent name.
    Therefore our only hope of drawing Him
    Is by reciting many different names;
    This Zoroaster did, the Sufis too.

Maga, Let us begin to watch the sacred Flame:
    The name that operates the miracle to-day
    Shall be his special message for the nonce.

Magus, First, he is Confessor of the Lost,
  Second, he is Minister to the Distressed,
  Third, he is Host to Lonely Souls,
  Fourth, he is Heir to all our Best Desires,
 Fifth, he is Helper to the Strugglers for the Right,
  Sixth, he is Artist of Beautiful Careers,
  Seventh, he is Watcher to Save us from Defeat,
  Eighth, he is Partner in every Task and Work,
  Ninth, he is Unlooser of every Problem's Knot,
  Tenth, he is the Leader of every Social Group,
  Eleventh, he is Silencer of every Sinful Voice,
  Twelfth, he is Apostle and Restorer of the Lost.
These are God's names for each month of the year.

Maga, To none of these does He respond to-day,
  So we must try the monthly Daily Name,
  Rehearsing first the First Week's Social Names.
  First of these names is Organizer of some Church,
  The second name is Peacemaker and Harmonizer
  The third name is Protector and Shepherd,
  The fourth name is Prophet and Seer,
  The fifth name is Healer of the Sick,
  The sixth name is Guide upon the Path,
  The seventh name is Teacher of the Ignorant.

Magus, To none of these does He respond to-day,
So we must try the second week's Familial Names,
  This first name is Father and Mother,
  This second name is Lover and Sweetheart,
  This third name is Bride and Bridegroom,
  This fourth name is Comrade in Solitude,
  This fifth name, Socratic, is Midwife,
  This sixth name is Hastener of Maturity,
  This seventh name is Messenger of Evangelistic
      Good News.

Maga, To none of these does He respond to-day,
So we shall try the third week's Occupational Names
Of which the first is Leader of this World's Orchestra,
The second name, Musician,
The third name is Painter,
The fourth name is Gardener,
The fifth name is Lawyer,
The sixth name is Physician,
While the seventh is Executioner and Embalmer!

Magus, To none of these does He respond to-day,
So we shall try the fourth week's Personal Names.
His first name is Oracle,
His second name is Solver of Problems,
His third name is Inspirer,
His fourth name is Hearer,
His fifth name is Discoverer,
His sixth name is Hierophant,
His seventh name is Miracle-worker.

Maga, To none of these does He respond to-day;
So we must try the fifth week's General Names,
Of which the first is Judge,
The second Redeemer and Savior,
The third Comforter, . .

Magus, Alas, to none of these does He respond to-day!
Mystus, Then we must give up hope of any help.
Mysta (to *Maga,*) Can you not think of any other name?

Maga, There is one more, — the rarest name of all,
The leap-year's single intercalary.
Mystus, Oh, let us try it!
Maga, Since the others failed,

FOURTH, *the VULTURE*

No doubt success this title will attend.
So for theophany let all prepare!
  (All gaze expectantly.)
Magus, Sweetest of all, our God is Heavenly Friend!
(A light thunder-clap, flowers are seen to fall, and from a distance are heard female voices singing)

THE HEAVENLY FRIEND

Dear Heavenly Friend, whom angel-hosts adore,
 Come, dwell with me, nor leave me evermore!

I have made room for thee, dear Heavenly Friend,
 Within the silence of my sanctuary,
 Where thou mayest come, and oft thyself unbend,
 And I may always find Divinity.

Come thou not only when with tears I pray,
 With thy most holy touch to comfort me,
 Stand near when earthly duties interfere,
 That while I labor I may gaze at Thee.

When I go out, be thou Companion mine,
 In every conversation take thou part;
 Deign thou to sit with me, and with me dine,
 And when I write inspire with heavenly art.

I would be always what I am sometimes
 When Thou art near me, and I taste thy grace;
 So stay with me through all my earthly times
 That I may steadfastly behold thy Face!

Dear Heavenly Friend, whom angel-hosts adore,
 Come, dwell with me, nor leave me evermore!

(During the hush that follows this, there appears the traditional face of *Jesus,* smiling, and seeming gently to utter,)

Jesus, My peace I leave unto you!
  (The light disappears.)

FOURTH, *the* VULTURE

Maga, O sacred Vultures and Iconoclasts,
 You see the God Supreme as Heavenly Friend,
 For only through his agency you know
 The nameless, formless, seven-fold Spirit-God
 Whom humans cannot name, unless they wrong
 Themselves, and fall into idolatry.
 Wherefore, when men shall ask your views of God,

Speak out, *One God, whose name is Character,*

Whose voice is Conscience, and his garments Facts;

Who incarnates as human Heavenly Friend.

Chorus. **We praise religious knowledge that leads to bliss,**

We praise God's Law, that swiftly reaches its goal,

And best will free us from dangers within;

Who is holy, clever, renowned, speedy to work,

Who works quickly, and cleanses well.

Rise up from thy seat, the Heavenly Mount!

Overtake me, O Law, that I may grow thine!

That all my thought, word, deed may be righteous,

Who transportest our souls to the heavens,

Revealing to us the highest mysteries,

Giving us strength for our worthiest work!

——— 1 ———

Questions to be Answered in Writing 🚩 4

Not to be answered all at once, but each on the indicated day of the month, overlapping from 22nd to 22nd.

The ideal time to study this Degree alone is in Nov. - December If the whole series is to be taken, it is best to begin on July 22.

But the first 22nd after you hear of these Degrees is the time Providence has set for *your* beginning; *anything* ranks delay.

DAY 22, Read and copy the Degree, and memorize your favorite selections therefrom, and record them.

Day 23, How does the *Vulture* typify Reformers?

Day 24, Enlarge on the significance of the *Seven Doves*, and which religions each characterizes.

Day 25, What reform did Zoroaster try to effect, and what happened to it?

Day 26, How can one best find the true name of God?

Day 27, Why is there no one single name of God true for all days?

Day 28, Comment on the various groups of divine names.

Day 29, Comment on the seven week-day divine names.

Day 30, Comment on the twelve monthly divine names.

Day 1, Comment on the seven divine names of the 1st, social week; 2nd, the familial; 3d, the congregational; 4th, the personal; 5th, the general.

Day 2, Which is the rarest and best name of God?

Day 3, Memorize and reproduce *the Heavenly Friend*.

Day 4, Give two reasons, one on God's side, and one on man's, why it is difficult to find God's true name.

Practical Experiments to be Reported ⚐ 4

Day 5, 6, Study the six ethnic religions mentioned in some good book (such as J. F. Clarke's *Ten Great Religions*,) and write out the 3 best points of each.

Day 7, 8, Read Edwin Arnold's *Pearls of the Faith*, and make up your own list of 30 divine names.

Day 9, 10, Get 30 beads, string them, write on each one of the names chosen, and prayerfully tell them over thrice a day. Note the effect on yourself. The Buddhists have done so for centuries.

Day 11, 12, Ask (not less than) a dozen non-Christian persons the grounds of their belief; and you will discover that the only differences between them result from vocabulary, race, geography and circumstances. It is hoped *your* faith will be founded on spiritual (but not spiritual*istic*) experiences.

Day 13, 14, List and interpret the seven Persian, and the Hebrew Archangels, and explain their importance for your life and career.

Day 15, 16, List the names given you by your relatives, friends and acquaintances; and study out what spiritual blessings are therefrom derivable; pray till you discover your *new name.*

Day 17, 18, Discover and list the points of agreement between the views of yourself and six other people belonging to organizations different from yours, on the 24 most important topics you can think of, and note the bearing of your results on the trend of public opinion of your times.

FIFTH DEGREE

The Ostrich

Valuation of Error.

The Mithraic Mysteries, Modernized.

Fifth Degree, the Ostrich

Major Points

1 **Symbol**, The Ostrich.
2 **Purpose**, To Find the Truth behind all Establtshed Systems.
3 **Scene,** The Mystery-tower fifth story.
4 **Peculiarity,** In some sense everybody is right.
5 **Temptation,** Respect due to age and position, the Hebrew Philosopher and the Gnostic Necromancer
6 **Oath,** To Fructify the Truth.
7 **Soul-part,** The Social Nature.

Minor Points

1 **Element,** Water.
2 **Sign,** Scorpio, or Reproductives.
3 **Planet,** Jupiter.
4 **Color,** Yellow.
5 **Flower,** Persica or Laurel.
6 **Jewel,** Ear-rings.
7 **Sign-parts**, Perseus, Eridanus, Lupus,

FIFTH DEGREE

The Ostrich, — Universality of Truth

(The Mystery-tower drop is let down the four stories, leaving but one showing, above which starts a bridge flying off into the clouds, to the right. In front of the central gates stretches a narrow balcony, setting off the gates' bas-reliefs of Jupiter, scorpions, broken columns, and reversed torches. The color is scarlet. To right and left two small wicket doors. The middle gates open sufficiently to allow the egress of the *Herald* and two figures, a *Jewish Philosopher* and *Gnostic Necromancer*, who sit down on seats between the central and wicket doors. When from the left the *Herald* blows, *Attendants* introduce *Mystus*, clad in purple, who seems rather frightened at the surroundings. The *Jewish Philosopher* beckons to him and says,)

Jewish Philosopher, What seekest thou?

Mystus, Advancement to new Truth.

Philosopher, The doors are draped in sable to denote
    Here is the end of initiation.

Mystus. Then why the higher floor, and then the
                              Bridge?

Philosopher, Wilt swear an oath of utter secrecy?

Mystus, I do!

(*Philosopher,* with eyes flashing, and in a mysterious tone,)

    The Bridge leads off into the clouds of Doubt;
    The highest secret is, *There is no Truth!*
    Beyond the letter of these Hebrew rolls,
    Whose every tittle is inerrantly
    Inspired by God, in revelation closed.
    To question aught is flagrant atheism;
    Kneel down and kiss it, and allegiance swear!

FIFTH, *the* OSTRICH

(Eight armed *Guards* come on, garbed and masked in black, their white eyes roll ominously through their masks.)

Mystus, But, Master, which edition is your scroll?
　　The manuscripts all differ thousand-fold;
　　Your texts lack points which meanings certify,
　　Reduplications, contradictions
　　Impossible, and low moralities,
　　Demand interpretation, at least.

Philosopher, Take, and go to heaven; or, leaving it,
　　Thy doom is an eternity of fire!

Mystus, My life a thousand times is forfeited
　　Whether I go or stay; so nought remains
　　But simply do what seems the right to me.
　　And whatsoe'er may seem its value true
　　It cannot pass at what your claims assert,
　　Inerrant, flawless, every jot and t!

Philosopher, Blasphemer! Your eternity is hell!
　　In spite of his own self, his soul to save,
　　Upon him, guards! Torture, till he recants!

Mystus, These guards all armed, they point me to my way:

Through them, not from them, must I turn my steps!
　　Here will I die to wrong, and live to Truth!

(*Mystus* fights, while a white-winged *Angel* shields him from blows, so he never has to fight more than one of the soldiers at a time, the others shouting and gesticulating. When one soldier is beaten down, the others carry him off. *Philosopher* disappears in a sulphurous cloud. *Mystus* picks up the soldier's discarded weapons, puts them on, and with the sword knocks at the wicket.)

Porter, [from within,] Who rudely dares disturb this sacred shrine?

Mystus, The Vulture MYSTUS, seeking further light.

Porter, What price have you to pay?

FIFTH, *the* OSTRICH

Mystus, My ear-rings may your sternness mollify.

(Receiving them through the wicket, and opening the door),
Porter, Enter in haste, for foes are threatening.

(Again the *Herald* blows his trumpet, and from the right is led in *Mysta,* blindfolded. She is led before the *Gnostic,* who says)

Gnostic, What seekest thou?

Mysta,   Advancement to new truth.
   Master, loosen the bandage, that I see!

Gnostic, Easier this Degree will be achieved
   By staying blindfold till your oath is sworn.
   Faith is the substance of the things you hoped,
   Wherefore the ignorant are chosen first
   For entrance to the Kingdom of the Lord;
   First take the vow, and then thou mayest look!
   Blindfold, you are preserved from scepticism.

(Tearing off the bandage,)

Mysta, My loving heart says yes, my mind says no:
   The God who made the eyes demands their use.
   Rather I'll go to hell with seeing eyes
   Since Paradise of Fools is really hell,
   Doomed to eventual disillusionment.

(On observing the *Gnostic Necromancer's* wizard-robe, and his Gnostic astrological chart of the Universe as described by Origen she shudders.)

Mysta, Such is the fate I narrowly escaped!
   Your costume is sufficient to inspire
   Distrust and fear. I hope you will explain
   That chart, with all its cabalistic signs!

Gnostic, In miniature it represents the world,
   Starting from BYTHOS, from which emanate
   Diverging lines of ÆONS seventy-two.

   This is the OGDOAD, from which SOPHIA fell,
  Whose tears achieved redemption for the race
  Through æons LIMIT, JESUS and the CROSS.
Mysta, I see, but do not fully understand
  How you these mysteries can have received.
Gnostic, Just as I told you, Child! It is always best
  To have recourse to faith, and not to sight;
  So many useless scruples will arise,
  That only make the Truth more hard to see.
Mysta, 'Faith' you are using for '*Docility;*'
  '*Faith*' means that we rely on God for help.
Gnostic, My daughter, this is not the place for doubts;
  These sable hangings show this is the end
  Of further progress in the Mysteries,
  Because mere knowledge of this mystic chart
  Confers salvation, so you cannot sin.
Mysta, And I might live whatever way I pleased?
Gnostic, Yes, for those who to it pledge their loyalty
  Have pow'r o'er any demons they might meet,
  Making them serve, by knowledge of their names.
Mysta, My conscience heretofore has been my guide;
  It sways my living loyalty entire,
  Which so I can't divert to any chart,
  Though I'm quite willing to make use of it.
  Besides, though this last revelation be,
  I would refuse return unto the world
  Until I penetrate the Tower Sixth,
  And fare along the Bridge into the clouds.
Gnostic, And from the clouds fall back upon the earth!
  Better remain in safety with the Truth.
Mysta, Answer me not, O Master, for I see
  Your answering soul spread darkness o'er your face
  As happens unto those who tell untruths.

FIFTH, *the* OSTRICH

Farewell, I pity you; may none be trapped!
The way that's opposite to yours is mine!

(*Black-robed maidens seek to draw her away; but she raises her hands and cries for aid. A white-robed* Angel *intervenes in her behalf. During an explosion, with a cry of rage, the* Gnostic *disappears; the* Black Maidens *flee, and* Mysta *knocks at the wicket.*)

Porteress, [from within,] Who dares disturb this sable sanctuary?

Mysta, Iconoclastic MYSTA, seeking light.

Porteress, What price have you to pay?

Mysta, Whate'er you ask.

Porteress, Those ear-ring pendants will as fee suffice.
(*Pushing them through the wicket,*)

Mysta, Take them at once, lest sometime I repent!

Porteress, [admitting her,] Hasten before the sacrament begins!

Chorus, From the regions of the cold rushed the deadly guileful Arch-fiend himself,
　Intent on preventing the revelation of the Truth.
So first he let loose on the Prophet the gloomy demon of death,
　But the Prophet heeded him not, engaged as he was in chanting his hymns of devotion:
In all discouragements profess the Law of Righteousness!
Disappointed, the demon sped back to the Arch-fiend:
　'I see no way to kill the Prophet while on his knees!'
Then the Prophet, who was looking into the mirror of his soul
　Beheld the Fiends in council plotting his death.
When the Arch-fiend realized that his schemes against the Prophet had failed, he groaned,
　'Myself I will go to tempt him away from the right

And manage somehow to distract him from prayer!'
So the Arch-fiend asked the Prophet riddles of grief and sin;
But the Prophet grew furious, and around his head swung the stones of his God:
'I will smite the worlds the Fiends have created
Their tricks and their senates, their books and their deeds.'

Whimpering the Arch-fiend pled for his race:
'Prophet, I beg you to spare me my children,
Were it not better to let them be servants?
Them will I give you, as also this beautiful Nature,—
All for a trifle, a minute of kneeling before me!'

With fury the faithfullest Prophet retorted:
·Why take as a gift from thy hand what myself I can conquer?'
The world that the Seven Archangels created,
The Law of the Lord, arising from dawn, will re-conquer!'

So the Prophet knelt down and resumed supplications:
'For this one only thing I ask of Thee, O Lord,—
Teach me Thy Truth, its mystery and power!'

(The Doors open, the altar is revealed, with the *Mages*. In front is chained an ostrich, who hides his head under his wings, and lies down. Behind the altar sits a masked, black-robed figure, wearing a conical cap and holding up an immense balance. The *Mystics*, blindfolded, wear fluffy ostrich-feather robes.)

Magus, Kneel down, and swear the oath of this degree.
Mystics, We swear we will be blind while judging truth,
Blind shall we be to all partiality;
We swear to adapt the truth that we have learned
So that the blind receive it with delight,
For the desirous ones reserving it.

FIFTH, *the* OSTRICH

    And as enlightened conscience will permit,
    To use all likely now existing means
    Without destroying any man's belief!

(The *Mystics* rise, and their bandages are removed. The ostrich, being goaded, also rises. From him each of the *Magi* draw one plume, and affixes it to one of the *Mystics*. Then *Magus* fastens laurel streamers around their breasts, and says,)

Magus, These laurel leaves, not only evergreen,
    But aromatic, luscious, bless mankind
    With heavenly renown; so do your lives
    Attractive with the rarest spice of heaven!

Maga, And so, dear Initiates, we say farewell!
    We pray you may your wishes realize,
    And whatsoe'er you may not understand
    You can supply by faith; farewell, Beloved!

(With evident signs of haste, the *Mages* wave farewell, and turn to leave, followed by their train. But the *Mystics* seem first puzzled, then anxious, and finally dissatisfied. So, suiting the actions to the words below, the *Mystics* halt the departing procession, which returns with a resigned expression, gradually assuming sufficient anxiety to appear annoyance, anger and apprehension and terror, expressed by trembling gestures.)

Mystics, Halt, halt! Return! We are not satisfied!

Mystus, We are not satisfied to rest in 'faith'
    As we have right to explications clear.

Magus, Many the rights whose granting is not wise.

Mysta, But this was the temptation just o'ercome,
    By 'faith' to be beguiled to what is false.

Maga, Not error only is the end of faith;
    There is much truth quite inexpressible.

Mystus, At any rate we'll hear what can be told!
    Why have we donned the robe of ostrich plumes?

Magus, Approached by enemies, the ostrich runs

FIFTH, the OSTRICH

      To hide his head beneath the desert sand.
      Useless is glare until the smoky glass
      Accommodates it to the human eye.

Maga, The ostrich lays his generous eggs in sand
      And trusts them unto God to hatch them out.
      So, Prodigals of Truth, leave it to God
      To fructify it to the Passer-by.

Magus, Till now you have sought Truth for your own sake;
      Now must you learn how it may fructify:
      A bitter struggle with the ignorant
      Who do not want the Truth, instinctively
      Destroying, crucifying their own Lord.

Mysta, What then is true enough for us to preach?

Maga, Puzzling indeed is this your weary task;
      The greatest sages here have made mistakes.
      There are no special rules by which to go,
      Each one must do his best upon this path.

Mystus, Why was the Scorpion symbol of this step?

Maga, Because the Truth, when over-definite,
      Breaks down, and stings whoever fondles it.

Mysta, But how were this the step of Jupiter
      When Scorpion's sting resumes its sacred lore?

Magus, Because the glorious shine of Jupiter
      Well symbolizes what all Truth should be;
      Not petty-fogging, not too much detailed,
      But fulgurating glory to all worlds.

Maga, So while that Hebrew scribe-philosopher
      Wrongly insisted on the script that kills,
      Yet was he right, demanding loyalty
      Unto the Scriptures certainly inspired
      By trailing spiritual glory-clouds.

Magus, The ethnic legends which therein are found

FIFTH, *the* OSTRICH

    Increase, more than diminish its authority,
    Making of it a handy summary
    Of all the great religions of the world,
    The most complete that e'er was given out,
    And in this sense the truest word of God.

Mysta, That would its contradictions well explain!

Mystus, The prophecies of really past events,
    Confusion from ambiguous Hebrew tense!

Mysta, And duplication of Creation-tales
    From Babylonian and Assyrian source!

Mystus, The Egyptian and Phœnician hero-lore!

Mysta, The universal Savior-incidents
    From Buddha, Krishna, realized in Christ!

Mystus, Tyanian Apollonius as a type!

Mysta, From Persian source the Archangelic lore!

Mystus, From Persia too the Resurrection-news!......

Magus, Now we have answered all you asked of us,
    We hope you will permit us to withdraw.
    The hour is late, there is great need of haste,—
    If now we leave, we still may safe remain!

Mystus, No, no! I still have doubts to be resolved!

Magus, Let us discuss them at some better time;
    Just now I feel as if some danger lowered.

Mysta, Evasions these, most unexpected here.
    Danger in sanctuary is impossible!

Maga, Even in Heaven there is a gate to Hell.

Mysta, Prove it!

Maga,   The archangel LUCIFER
    From Heaven was hurled to lowest pits of Hell;
    Therethrough Lord JESUS visited the hells,
    Therethrough the damned at last shall be reclaimed.

Mysta, Perhaps you may be right; but we are safe

      In practising what put our foe to flight;
      Wherefore I shall continue asking Truth.
      Explain the chart of that necromancer!
Maga, Although that Gnostic wisdom was all wrong
      Pretending to divulge all mysteries,
      That sage was right, insisting on the depths
      Of unseen Wisdom's piloting decrees.
Magus, Only, the Truth is greater than all words,
      Greater than any vision of To-day;
      His chart was true, if merely tentative;
      But false as limit, as restraining chain.
Mystus, Why is the color of this step all black?
Mysta, Who is that sable form, holding the scales?
Maga, To bid you both prepare for next Degrees,
      Where in most real sense you both shall die
      Unto the old surroundings where you lived,
      And shall begin another kind of life
      Where limitations shall have passed away.
Mystics, Why were our earrings the admission fee?
Magus, Still further queries? Expensive is Truth!
Mysta, And is there anything that we have spared?
      Have we not paid full price at every step?
Maga, Oh yes, but higher still are further fees.
Mystics, Mention the price, and we will not hold back!
Magus, (with resignation,) Those ear-rings symbol-
                      ized external things.
      Henceforth beneath the surface must you look
      For the significance of thoughts and words,
      For destiny of self and of the world.
Maga, Henceforth you shall discover everywhere
      An esoteric wisdom heavenly,
      And listen for the beating of the heart
      Of this external universe of worlds.

FIFTH, *the* OSTRICH

For lo, this heart is the interior truth
That shines in words, and flashes in our dreams,
So that they utter better than they know
When their internal ears are listening
For revelations from the spirit-land.
These are the ornaments that suit your ears,
And not bejeweled pendants, gold-encased.

Magus, Wherefore approach, I will baptize your ears
   By whispering in them the mystic name
  Which shall, if rightly whispered, open heaven.

Mystus, (boastfully,) Just see how well we did to
                           insist on Truth!

Mysta, How terrible it is we so are tried
   We never know whose counsel we can trust!
    On scepticism our sole success depends!

(Horror freezes all into motionless statues at a sudden pandemonium. All the doors are burst in, and the sanctuary is invaded by a carnival of demons led by *Father Time* with hour-glass and scythe, followed by the labeled *Spirits of Every Annual Festival*, including *Mardi-Gras, Ash Wednesday, St Valentine's Day,* etc, who with warlike shouts throw themselves on the *Mages & Mystics,* who have no time to defend themselves before they are bound, and by their wrists are chained to rings on panels on the central altar. In the meanwhile, with a cracked voice, *Father Time* calls all his train to attention. By the hand he holds a masked ghost-like figure wearing around the chest a phosphorescent band showing in fiery letters, *Hallowe'en.* The demon-crew keeps up blood-curdling yells.)

Time, Attention, Children, Festivals and Fasts!
   This is Walpurgis-night, or Hallowe'en,
    To-night we crown the Vigil of All Souls.
    To-night rules he, to-night he sways the world,
To-night his message speaks the Most High's mind;
   Now let us bow before his short-lived power!

(Cheering, cries of *Long live All Souls!* Wild dancing by all the characters mentioned below, and witches with brooms, sorcerers with wands, ghosts, bats and black cats.   Everything stops as *Hallowe'en* stands forth and holds out his sceptre.)

Hallowe'en, Spirits, I have survived the centuries,
    Religions rise and fall, and still I rule.
    To-night I liberate the slaves of Hell,
    The Universe is creaking on its hinge;
    Come, ye forgotten souls, and ye oppressed!

Shamans, Long since extinct, we Shamans still attempt
    To fructify Australian destiny.

Medicine Men, When sick, the Indians on my skill rely;
    By noise the evil spirits I drive off.

Djinns, The desert hillocks dance before my breath;
    All straggling souls I call to Mecca's Stone.

Trolls, The snowy polar fields have many cracks
    From which the unwary I attempt to save.

Devs, I love to slay the mild producing cow,
    With nomads, settlers' pastures I ride down.

Hindu Demons, The Hindus tremble when we plague the sick,
    When luck is adverse, when the wicked weep.

Furies, We follow liars, thieves and murderers,
    Pursuing those who have committed crimes.

Mummies, The Nile brings down much blessing and much curse,
    We linger in the crypts of pyramids.

Poulpiquets, We torture those who fail in daily tasks,
    We tease the children, and we poison wells.

All, This Witches' Sabbath strengthens tyranny
    By slowing progress of democracy.

Hallowe'en,   Thanks, loyal friends, for gathering round me
    But I desire the presence of your chiefs.

FIFTH, *the* OSTRICH

(As *Hallowe'en* points to each one, the latter leaves the crowd, comes forward, declaims his line, and takes his place in a seated circle around *Hallowe'en*.)

    LOKI am I, who tempted Asgard's Gods!

    I, ANGRA-MAINYU, Zoroaster mocked!

    SATAN am I, the one who tempted Job!

    AZAZEL I, in desert punished Jews!

    ABADDON I, who tempted Anthony!

    APOLLYON I, who tempted Jesus Christ!

Earth's kings drugged I, BABYLON, scarlet whore!

Hallowe'en, Thank you indeed, my trusted councillors
    Who here have gathered to renew your youth.
    You are the keenest messengers of God
    To sift what's genuine from cloaked pretense,
    To keep all souls unworthy out of heaven.
    Now, here before you stand two initiates
    Chained so that from your wiles they cannot flee,
    As they insisted on awaiting you —
    Many a grief is saved to such as haste!
    Perhaps examination they would like.
    MYSTUS, which one of these Examiners
    Would you prefer, to certify your weal?
    Loki, or Satan, or Apollyon sly,
    Or Babylon, the mystic scarlet whore?

(Pale, with beads of cold perspiration upon his brow, stammering)

Mystus, From all temptation, Lord, deliver us!

Hallowe'en, Such worthy prayer is sheer hypocrisy
  From one who warnings scorned, and who remained
    To force himself into temptation's maw.
    Now, MYSTA dear, you too shall make your choice
    From Angra-Mainyu, Abaddon, Azazel;
    Whom do you choose as an Examiner?

(Suddenly transformed as a handsome youth, clad in purple, a flower chaplet on his brow, and a wine-cup in his hand. Hic-coughing, he sneeers,

Angra-Mainyu, MYSTA, my darling, give me just one
                                            kiss!

(Dropping his robe and appearing as a girl garbed in yellow, he throws his arms around *Mysta,* and presses his body on hers,)

Abaddon, Chum of my heart, let us be each others'
                                            slaves!

(Suddenly transformed into an angel, except that his face remains black,)

Azazel, Alluring soul-mate, let us celebrate
      Interior Respiration's sacrament!

Mysta, (sobbing), Out of the depths of sin, which I
                                          deserved,
      Hear my complaint, and rescue me at once!

(There are heard six strokes of a bell, cocks crow, dawn breaks, and a rain-bow appears. Led by *Father Time,* there appears *Dawn,* rosy-fingered and saffron-garbed. Without effort she breaks through the central doors. The *Chorus,* the *Tempters* and *Hallowe'en* groan, growl, hiss and make wild gestures, but seem to be invisibly driven away. *Hallowe'en* disappears last, expostulating with *Father Time,*)

Hallowe'en, O Father TIME, how fickle are thy smiles!
      One hour past you crowned me king of all,
      But now I'm driv'n before another pow'r!

Time, God's pow'r is founded on progressiveness;
      Blest is the man who tastes each moment's bloom,
      New every morn is immortality!

(With loud scolding gradually subsiding into plaintive gibbering the *Shades* disappear. As *Dawn* grows more dazzling, *Time* leads her away. At the door she looks back with a heavenly smile. As she leaves the rainbow disappears into full day-light. The *Mystics* wipe their forehead, breathe deeply, look around, and pinch themselves to make sure they are awake.)

FIFTH, *the* OSTRICH

(When *Dawn* had first come in she had, by a stroke of her wand, caused the chains of the *Mystics & Mages* to fall off with a clanking noise,)

Magus, Come, let us thank our God for morning joy!

All, We praise thee, O God! We acknowledge thee
                              to be the Lord!
All the earth doth worship thee, the Father universal!

(*Mysta* still seems to have something on her mind. Tenderly *Maga* encourages her to come out with it.)

Maga, Your sweet unanswered thought, my dear,
                              speak out!

Mysta, I am confused, and though afraid to ask,
    I still would hear the pass-word mystical
      You were about to give, when Hell broke loose!

Maga, I think you need not have me tell it you;
    No doubt you guessed it in your hour of need.

Mystus (with joy in his eye), *Our God is conscience!*

Mysta,   *And his Voice is dreams!*

             (Nodding approval,)

Maga, Farewell! Guard well the chain around your
                                  neck,
    Lest in the next Degree you fail, and die!

Magus, But ere you go, my Children, let me place
    Upon your brows a wreath of laurel leaves
      Culled from the *persica,* an evergreen,
    These leaves are good to eat; they have a taste,
    A fine aroma, like an eastern spice.
    It bears a fruit, of stony heart indeed,
    But luscious, like the sweetest of all pears.
    Such be your life, dear Children, in the world,
    Forever green, with heavenly renown!

——— m. ———

Questions to be Answered in Writing 🖋 5

Not to be answered all at once, but each on the indicated day of the month, overlapping from 22nd to 22nd.

The ideal time to study this Degree alone is in Oct. - November If the whole series is to be taken, it is best to begin on Aug. 22.

But the first 22nd after you hear of these Degrees is the time Providence has set for *your* beginning; *anything* ranks delay.

DAY 22, Read and copy the Degree, and memorize your favorite selections therefrom, and record them.

Day 23, In what way was the Jewish philosopher wrong, and in which way was he right?

Day 24, In what way was the Gnostic necromancer wrong, and in which way was he right?

Day 25, Give an acconnt of the celebrated Temptation of Zoroaster.

Day 26, What is the initiatory significance of the Ostrich?

Day 27, What is the initiatory significance of the Laurel?

Day 28, What is the initiatory significance of the Scorpion?

Day 29, What is the initiatory significance of the planet Jupiter?

Day 30, What is the initiatory significance of the Ear-rings?

Day 1, In judging external definitions of the Truth, what is the difference between the fool's, and the sage's attitudes.

Day 2, What is the best preliminary definition of Truth?

Day 3, Is there any expectation that interior listening can ever be dispensed with? Why?

Day 4, To what does the real Truth always lead?

Practical Experiments to be Reported 🕮 5

Day 5, 6, Make out a list of statements that are litterally true, but substantially false, such as are many advertisements.

Day 7, 8, Make out a list of statements that are litterally false, but substantially true, such as the rough and ready expressions of the unreflecting.

Day 9, 10, Make out a scheme of how to adapt the same truth to six very different people, as salesmen have to do.

Day 11, 12, Make a list of the reasons why six different men voted for the same candidate.

Day 13, 14, Collate the expressions of great scientists on the impossibility of final definition of Truth [as in Fiske's *Idea of God*, or Stewart & Tait's *Unseen Universe*.]

Day 15, 16, Make a list of five imperfections of the Bible, and its five best points, noting the profounder importance of the latter.

Day 17, 18, Collate [from some *History of Philosophy* such as Schwegler's] the *categories* or chief principles of the Hindus, Greeks, Plato, Aristotle, the Stoics, Spinoza, Kant, Hegel, and of each chief religion.

Day 19, 20, Make a list of your own 12 most important *categories*, or principles, truths, or classifications of things existing; and define their interrelation, which is called *God*.

SIXTH DEGREE

The Raven

Judgment of Self-knowledge

The Mithraic Mysteries, Modernized.

Sixth Degree, the Raven.

Major Points

1 **Symbol**, The Raven.
2 **Purpose**, Judgment.
3 **Scene**, The summit of the Mystery-tower, and the Flying Bridge leading off into space.
4 **Peculiarity**, Success depends on the first practical achievement, voluntary illumination of the feet.
5 **Temptation**, Irresponsible cancellation of the Past.
6 **Trial**, The Tower is on fire, and escape depends on using their coffins as bridges.
7 **Oath**, Silence of Pleasures and Passions.
8 **Soul-part**, The Conscience.
9 **Divisions**, 1, Introductory Feast; 2, Judgment; 3, Revelation of Identity of Judges. 4, Trial.

Minor Points

1 **Element**, Water.
2 **Sign**, Libra, or the Kidneys.
3 **Sign-parts**, Corvus, Spica, Ursa Major.
4 **Planet**, Saturn.
5 **Color**, Gold.
6 **Flower**, Double Banana Leaf.
7 **Jewels**, Necklace and Hair-fillet.

SIXTH DEGREE

The Raven, — Judgment

I, Introduction.

(The Temple-gardens. Tables are set for a banquet. The *Mystics* have just finished their repast, and servants are removing everything but the fruit and wine.)

Mystus, Being apostles of the sacred Truth
    We should, by common sacrament of cheer,
    Cement the bonds of friendship of our souls
    In intervals between the sacred rites.

Mysta, Loosening relations terrestrial
    We should improve celestial fellowship;
    And realizing God is common Sire
    We recognize our common family.

(Suddenly there is heard sad trumpet-music. There appear four *Musicians* introducing a *Masked Figure* garbed in black, bearing a torch, followed by four more, carrying a small coffin containing a mummy, followed by four singers intoning the following)

Dirge, All hail, Good Man, fated to pass away!
    Hirers of houses no longer shall have houses to hire;
    Bards have sung, 'What is prosperity?'
    No one ever returned from thence to recount
    Their words or doings, to encourage their hearts;
    For you go to the place whence there is no return.
    Distract your heart by wild enjoyment,
    Anoint your head, array yourself in finest linen,
    Fulfil all your desires while life holds good, —

But the day shall come when thy voice shall grow mute:
Lamentations deliver not him who has gone down to the tomb,
No one who has gone thither has ever returned,
No one can carry away his goods with him.

We sing to the wisdom that comes from telling the truth
And utters the warnings of rectitude,
For while summer inspires the bards to sing
And paints all their plumage with colors gay,
In sable arrayed, unmoved, unloved,
The Raven reminds of the ever-returning autumn-truth.

We sing the opinions of the Spirit of Wisdom
Through the powerful, calm repose of the Angels,
Those princely, purpose-fulfilling sages.
They are the best of all helpers for the getting of wisdom
Through largely acquiring both reason and thought
Innate in the soul from the fountains of truth
For the perfect management of worldly and spiritual undertakings
In wisdom acquired experimentally through hearing and thought.

Henceforward with zeal we shall celebrate
Wisdom's weird liturgy and sacrament
In which Wisdom's nurture we may receive;
For to our litanies Wisdom shall clearly appear,
Offering to be our guide in shaping our bodily career,
And preparing our soul for life in the spirit-land!

(As the procession reaches the *Mystics*, *Mystus* tries to avoid it; but its *Leader* demands recognition.)

Leader, Kneel and salute, if you would have us pass.

(*Mystus* does so, and the *Leader* does the same with *Mysta*. Then the procession leaves, whereupon says)

Mystus, Let us proceed with our sweet feast of love;
Permitted, nay, commanded by the priests!

SIXTH, *the* RAVEN

Mysta, If short our life, so much the more we need
  New power from the marriage of our souls.
Mystus, With joy I sing the pæan of To-day;
  Take all the prophecies, give me the acts;
  Dreamers are shamed before the invincible......

(A *Chorus* sings the xith Chapter of *Ecclesiastes,* when the procession returns; but the coffins that it carries this time are large, and silently *Attendants* attack the *Mystics* and force each one of them into one coffin, they having been pulled down by their necklaces, being gagged, masked, and having their hands bound.)

2, Judgment.

(The large doors of the Mystery-tower. All is black, adorned with the symbols of Saturn, and scales. Into the clouds on the right leads a Flying Bridge, from the roof, near a small domed gilt pavilion. There in front of the closed gates sit twelve black-masked *Judges,* on seats behind small altars. As the gong sounds midnight there are heard three heavy knocks at the small left end door at the head of the stairs leading up from the stage-level).

Magus, Who seeks to enter in this grim abode?
Maga, Who dares the threshold of the gate of death?
Priest, (through the lattice,) Two Ostriches who would
  advancement find.
Magus, And have they paid the price of further light?
Priest, Each one has paid the heavy price of growth,
  And here their necklaces are handed you.
Maga, Are both prepared as will the work befit?
Priest, Within their coffins are their scarlet robes.
Magus, Their arms?
Priest,   In resignation crossed upon their breasts.
Maga, Their eyes?
Priest,   By sable bandage rendered blind.

Magus, Which one comes first?

Priest, The Ostrich MYSTUS here,
Who cries for judgment to the Mind of God.

Maga, Advance, and bring him in before his Judge!

Attendants, Oh pray for wisdom to the Judge supreme!

Magus, Which one comes next?

Priest, The Ostrich MYSTA next,
Who cries for judgment to the Heart of God.

Maga, Advance, and introduce her to her Judge!

Attendants, Oh pray for vision to the Judge of all!

(The *Mystics* are released. Silence, thunder and lightning. Standing in their coffins, they cry for Judgment,)

Mystus, I claim a Judgment!

Mysta, A Judgment I demand!

(An *Attendant* gives incense to the *Mystics.* As soon as it is thrown on the altar of the respective Judge, the latter, in sepulchral tones, booms out,)

Judge, Confess your mortal sin!

Mystus, It is caprice.

Mysta, 'Tis cowardice of heart.

Judge, What ruling motive influenced your life?

Mystus, Insistence on mere niceness of each thing.

Mysta, In each relationship, I sought for love.

Judge, What trait of character did you despise?

Mystus, Dullness I hated most, and fled from it.

Mysta, The self-assertive most repulsive seemed.

Judge, Are you desirous to amend your life?

Mystus, I would become by far more exquisite.

Mysta, That is my effort, even in my dreams.

Judge, Then call high Heaven as witness to this oath!

SIXTH, *the RAVEN*

Mystus, Silence of pleasure I now undertake,
   The thought of coming death shall sober me,
   Accuracy shall become my guiding star,
   My sense shall harmonize with things divine.

Mysta, Silence of passions henceforth I observe,
   My words shall naught but rectitude express,
   Endurance is the pole by which I steer,
   Cooperation I shall show to be divine.

Judges, Hail, mystic Ravens, human and divine!

(*Attendants* cover the *Mystics* with mantles of ravens' feathers, and fix in their hair the double banana leaf. Their coffins are turned over, and they are made to stand on them; it is then seen that to their backs are affixed heavy packs; their arms are crossed, their heads are bowed.)

Chorus, The Sage asked the Spirit of Wisdom,
   'Through how many ways and motives do people mostly arrive in Heaven?'

The Spirit of Wisdom thus answered the Sage:

The first good work is liberality, then truth, thankfulness, contentment, friendliness, faith, opposition to evil, belief in immortality, marrying to save the race, adopting orphans, and industry.

The second grade of good works is religiousness, considerateness, good reputation, lovableness, charitable, retiring, chaste, loving concord, piously arranging the wills of the dead, without wrath, and brave under adversity.

The third grade of good works is not being lazy, belief in holy beings, in Judgment leading to heaven and hell, freedom from slander, progressiveness for self and others, defending the good and accusing the bad, free from deceit, veracious, true to promises, reforming others, and furnishing lodgings for the sick and the strangers.

These are the thirty-three good works that lead to Heaven.

3, Revelation *of the* Judges.

(Suddenly the central doors open, revealing the altar, brightly illuminated. Near it stand the *Mages*. Organ-music, thunder.)

Magus, Before you can be welcomed, Children dear,
    Not only must each one of you be judged,
    But each must from his Judge receive his cross;
  Wherefore step forwards most courageously.

(Diffidently each of the *Mystics* approaches his own judge, *Mystus* the *Mind-Judge*, *Mysta* the *Heart-Judge*. They kneel and plead, but in vain. At last they snatch their crowns out of their Judges' hands, and put them on. From within sounds a triumphal trumpet-march.)

Magus, Know ye, that since the world was made for man,
No man was crowned, but that he crowned himself,
    The heavenly kingdom suffering violence;
So that unless yourselves had snatched the crowns
    They had not self-control on you conferred.
    But more is needed; ere you can approach,
  You must have seen the face of your own Judge;
    For none may enter, ere he tell to us
    What likeness he beheld beneath that veil.

(The doors close upon the altar and the *Mages*. After hesitation, in hopes of leading the two Judges to speak, the *Mystics* throw incense on the Judges' altarlets. A thick cloud rises, into which rush the *Mystics* to raise the Judges' veils. Sharp cries, thuds, crashes are heard. When the cloud rises, the *Mystics* are discerned lying insensible on the floor; they revive slowly. The 12 Judges have disappeared, and in their place yawns an abyss separating the *Mystics* from the large Doors, which slowly open revealing the illuminated sanctuary with the *Mages*, trumpet-blowing priests, and a winding stair-way leading to the pavilion on the roof.)

SIXTH, *the* RAVEN

Maga, Quickly come here; do you not see the fire?
(Looking back towards the front of the stage, the *Mystics* see that the lower stories of the Tower seem to smoke, and flames ascend. The floor sags; confusion.)

Mystus, We must jump down!

Mysta,   The distance is too great!

Mystus, I could, without the burden of this pack.
        (Stretching forth her hand to the *Mages,*)

Mysta, Your help we both implore!

Magus, The only help is that which lies in you.
   Yourselves are your own saviors, and your gods.
    Ravens should know how over holes to fly.

(The *Mystics* consult; finally they use their coffins as bridges, but none too soon, as the whole front of the Tower crashes in, replaced by smoke and fire. As the *Mystics* look into this vertiginous abyss they grow pale and tremble.)

Maga, MYSTICS, refrain from dangerous delay;
   Even this central portion is on fire,
   And not until you have achieved success
   Could you escape; wherefore declare at once
   What you beheld beneath your judges' veils.

Mystus, I saw my face as when I was a child;
   It was *my better Self* who was my judge!

Mysta, I saw myself as I have wished to be,
   Possessed of my own heart, radiant and brave.

Mages, This lesson learn: *Your Conscience is your god!*

(As if to emphasize the sacredness of this revelation, there burst forth the following *Choruses* (the Zoroastrian Lord's Prayer, the *Ashem Vohu,* the *Ahuna-Vairya,* and other Glorias) from different directions, each one having seemed to be the last. Meanwhile the terrified *Mystics,* urged on by the growing fire and explosions, by gestures and utterances show they consider this otherwise praise-worthy devotion ill-timed, and even positively dangerous, but they do not dare to stop it by violence.)

The ASHEM VOHU

The will of the Lord is the law of holiness;
Unto him who, according to God's Will,
Wields God's God-given power to relieve the Poor
Shall be given the duplex riches of a noble mind:
Brightness and glory, vigor and health,
Welfare and energy, and long eternal life,
Below; and when he shall pass beyond, he shall achieve
That bright and happy, blissful home of saints!

The YATHA AHUNA VAIRYO

May God be rejoiced by those who do His utmost wish!
Embracing all good thoughts, words and deeds,
Praying to the Seven Archangels from fullness of heart,
And at need sacrificing his life for the good of the poor!
Holiness is the best of all goods!
Which holiness itself may approach perfection
For sacrifice, prayer, propitiation and glorification,
Unto God the holy, and Master of holiness.

4, *The* Trial.

(Thunder and lightning. Suddenly pieces of the ceiling and floor fall, so as to make room for an immense balancing scale, each one of whose pans fits into its appropriate hole in the floor. In the left hand scale lie the six jewels given up by the *Mystics* as entrance fees at each Degree. The other scale-pan is large enough for one of the Candidates to step on. The balances tremble considerably. The only light comes through the holes in floor and ceiling. There appear black robed and masked *Figures* standing by the scales, in their hands holding stylus and tablet. Another one lays on the altar an immense book labeled *Book of Doom*, which he solemnly opens; its pages are phosphorescent.)

SIXTH, *the* RAVEN

Magus, Serious are these complications now;
    What you thought an ordeal, was no more
    Than preparation for this Judgment true.
    These jewels are the symbols of your life,
    And show that what you gave away stays yours
    While what you kept you probably shall lose.

Maga, Your planetary progress up this Tower
    Consisted of one portion of your soul
    Each time explored, redeemed and perfected.

    First was the silver Moon of anklets low,
    The horse-like body-facts on which you ride.

    Second, of Mercury the bracelets gilt
    Symboled control of that fierce bull of sleep,
    That part of you that has desires and appetites.

    Third was the topaz belt that Venus meant,
    Where all your senses' joys were disciplined
    By beating down the Lion of Disease.

    Horse, Bull, Lion, — three animals of earth,
    That symbolized your preparation for
    Successful wrestling for the earthly crown.

    Continuing through the planetary worlds
    The journey of the growing human Soul,
    Fourth was the breast-pin gift of purple Mars,
    The manly courage of the Vulture's swoop
    Destroying all that separates God's folk.

    Fifth were the ear-rings of red Jupiter,
    Prodigal as the Ostrich, that the Truth,
    Accommodated to the hearers, grow;
    This symbolized your social element.

    Sixth, the necklaces of Saturn black
    Describe the spiritual conscience-realm,
    Symbolized by the Raven's warning croak.

So, having passed through Earth, you were prepared

To go through air as Vulture, Ostrich, Raven;
Which realm of air you now will leave behind,
And by the Judgment Bridge you see above
Pass to the realms of astral mystery, —
Which heaven is no more than your own best self.

This journey through the planetary worlds
Thus symbolized the sevenfold human soul:
Body, desire, senses, emotions, mind,
Socialness, conscience, thus the tale is told;
Each one of which, now perfected, prepares
Further ascent to six-fold spirit-realm.

Magus, Wherefore those jewels six there represent
All of your life so far; should they outweigh
All that is mortal yet contained in you,
Up shall you swing into the Judgment Hall,
And be admitted to the Flying Bridge
O'er which if you can fare successfully
Unto the Mount of Vision you shall reach.

Maga, But if the mortal yet a part of you
Outweighs the jewels in the other scales,
Yourselves may judge where you at last shall land.

(She points to the darkness in the holes; she throws down a pebble, and the splash is heard only after a long while. The *Mystics* shudder and shriek.)

Wherefore you first must rid you of those packs
Since e'en without them you may not survive.
Why do you not obey?

Mystus,   I cannot loosen it.

Mysta, Had I a knife!

Mages, And right you are! You cannot throw them off,
They are the errors of your life entire;
No arm of flesh could tear them off from you,
And yet they doom your soul to sure defeat.

SIXTH, the RAVEN

    What will you do?

Mysta, Ask you to take them off.

Maga, That may not be; for do you not suppose
  Had I the power, you had long since been freed?

(Thunder; the balances sway. Holding out a cross to them to kiss, says a highly ornamented)

Bishop, Kiss but this cross, your sins are all forgiven!

Mysta, Forgiveness I refuse; I pay my way!

Bishop, Then shall you die in midst of all your sins!

Mystus, Although forgiven, myself would not forgive!

Mysta, How could forgiveness hush my conscience-cry?

Maga, Nobly, my children, have you stood the test;
    Although someone your burdens could remove,
    You would refuse to part with them by trick.

Mysta, (as if inspired), I see it writ in flames:
    'Repent, confess in public, you are freed!'
    Secret confession is but false pretense;
    However sinful, if I publish all,
    No further claim the Universe can hold.

(She approaches the *Recorder*, returns his glare, seizes his tablet, turns aronnd, and starts to read. But she hesitates and blushes, still she gets hold of herself, and firmly proceeds),

    'Envy and anger, laziness and pride,'—
    If more there is, God, bring it back to me!

(With an explosion, her pack rolls off into her scale-pan, and rolls down the hole. She herself then springs onto the scale-pan which though it trembles does not spring up. This makes her anxious.)

Mysta, O God, what shall I do? if even now,
    When all has been confessed, I cannot rise!

(She bursts into tears, *Maga* whispers to her; into the scale-pan she throws her golden hair-fillet. The balance-scale then throws her upwards, and she would have disappeared but that *Magus* holds her down.)

Magus, Delay a moment, while I paint the way.
  Up there sits GOD, whose angels drive the soul
  Into the darkness of the Razor-bridge
  That leads to shores of which we dare not speak.
  There is no light, but what each neophyte,
  By taking thought, can kindle in his feet.
  Who learned it, will pass on; who learned it not
  Finds it too late, and falls into the Pit.
  Now, all together, pray until she glows!

(They all breathe, directing their power by pointing their fingers successively at each of the 12 vital parts of *Mysta*. She glows, the scale-pan in which she stands ascends. She disappears below, but reappears on the Bridge, and through the clouds her shining feet gleam the last of her).

Maga, Now, MYSTUS, you may try the Razor-bridge!
Mystus, I will not go; I am afraid; the risk is great.
Maga, Where woman has succeeded, why not you?
Mystus, Women will blindly rush where men reflect;
  Still, I will try, relying on God's help.

(*Mystus* goes through the confession. The audience prayerfully breathes and assists his transfiguration; he throws the circlet on the other scale-pan, he is shot up, he reappears on the Bridge. He is seen to waver; he falls with a thud. *Priests* run to him, and through his lips force Lethe-water, so he might forget the initiation, and try again next year. Then *Camillus*, also bearing a pack on his back, goes through the same rites and passes over the Bridge successfully. He is a neophyte who had failed the year before. The following *Chorus* is heard in the meanwhile.)

I

When a soul departs this life, where spends she that night?

She sits near the body's head, singing hymns of joy;
For three nights she tastes all the pleasures of the living world.

At the end of the third night, when the dawn appears,

SIXTH, *the* RAVEN

The soul is brought amid fragrant plants
Where blows a breeze from southern gardens, to meet
Its Conscience in the guise of a fifteen year old girl,
Fair, vivacious, white-armed, slender and glad.

II

'O Youth of good thoughts, good words and good deeds,
Who askest my name, I am thine own Conscience;
To me thou appearest as lovely as I to thee;
And when thou chantest hymns, or feedest the poor
Through thy good thoughts and speeches and deeds
Lovely though I am, thou makest me still more radiant,
Till thou worship me for having communion with God.'

III

Then the first step of that good soul ushered it into
the Good Thought Paradise;
Its second step, into the Good Word Paradise,
Its third step, into the Good Deed Paradise,
Its fourth, into the intelligible light of the Mount Serene.

IV

There that good soul was asked by some of the Blessed,
'Dear Saint, do describe your experiences of departure!'
But the Lord will remonstrate, 'Ask not this of him
Who has just emerged from the paths of Fear and Distress
Rather give him the Food of Heaven, the sacred butter;
This is the proper food for souls of good thoughts, of
good words, and good deeds!'

V

Ye gods full of glory and healing, but trembling
At the fragrance exhaled by the righteous soul
Who seizes the heavenly reward as promptly
As a wolf would throw itself on defenseless sheep
Manifest your greatness by giving gifts to the law-abiding
Hear me, forgive me! Yes, I hear you thunder:
'We, the Archangels will come and show the way
To the World Above, to the long Glory in Paradise,
To the Knowledge-God's Mountain of Serene Abode;
And when Fate shall draw his soul from his body,
I, the Lord of Wisdom, when he asks for it,
Will gently show him his destined abode,
And impart to him the full blessing of Heaven!'

Questions to be Answered in Writing ✍ 6

Not to be answered all at once, but each on the indicated day of the month, overlapping from 22nd to 22nd.

The ideal time to study this Degree alone is in Sept to October If the whole series is to be taken, it is best to begin on Sept 22 But the first 22nd after you hear of these Degrees is the time Providence has set for *your* beginning; *anything* ranks delay.

Day 22, Read and copy the Degree, and memorize your favorite selections therefrom, and record them.

Day 23, Why did MYSTUS fall, and MYSTA not fall?

Day 24, Study the *halo* in Zoroastrian and Christian religions, the Bible, art, and lives of the Saints.

Day 25, Study the *intelligible light* in St Clement of Alexandria, and Plotinus. Start the practical work.

Day 26, What means the planetary tower-progress?

Day 27, Explain the meaning of the six jewels, the soul-parts, the symbols of the work up to here.

Day 28, Mention your own chief failing, your ruling motive, your own most despicable trait, and the traits you most admire and despise.

Day 29, Which means failed in removing the soul-burden, and which succeeded?

Day 30, What four steps lead to Paradise?

Day 1, What decides whether or not the soul is raised in the scales?

Day 2, Why could not the soul advance until it told the name of the Veiled Judge?

Day 3, What kind of false Christianity is meant by the false bishop?

Day 4, What was in the kiosk, above the stage, and what started from there?

Practical Experiments to be Reported 🏴 6

Day 5, 6, Write out your own catalogue of 42 good works, organizing them by three increasing grades, and then study the contrast between both lists.

Day 7, 8, List your friends, and define the kind of friendship that brought you together, and that which keeps you together; read Cicero's *Friendship*

Day 9, 10, List the people who dliske you, or disapprove of you; make them define the reasons of their disapproval.

Day 11, 12, Write out a careful self-examination, for convenience using the Progressive Membership Circular classification.

Day 13, 14, If you have done any wrong, atone for it as well as you can, if possible to the wronged person; or if that person has passed out of your sphere, pass the satisfaction on to somebody else.

Day 15, 16, If you have any secret sin on your conscience, confess it to your best friend, and observe your own relief, following that confession (it does not matter *to whom* — and it had better *not* be a priest who *imagines* he has the exclusive right to grant or withhold absolution; nor to the assembly of your future associates, as do the Shakers.) The object of confession is not to hinder you by putting yourself in the power of interested parties, but to help you by affording you relief, by demonstrating to you that *confession constitutes absolution*, and therefore is the divine method of forgiveness. That is why so many women do so much talking; it is a relief.

Day 17, 18, By daily practice, culminating to-day bring to your feet a sensation of heat. This is accomplished by thinking of Divine Light while inhaling, and then continuing the breath-sensation down into the feet while exhaling.

SEVENTH DEGREE

The Griffin

Vindication of Divine Justice.

The Mithraic Mysteries, Modernized.

Seventh Degree, the Griffin.

Major Points

1 **Symbol**, The Griffin.
2 **Purpose**, To justify our lot in life.
3 **Scene**, The Telestic Cave, where is made the search for the Lost Master-Word in Life.
4 **Peculiarity**, The secret was present all the time, and needed no more than to be gathered and ordered.
5 **Temptation**, To doubt God's Justice, and to scorn misplaced fragments.
6 **Oath**, To trust God's Justice, and to use this knowledge only for Consolation, Inspiration and Blessing, and not for Procrastination, imaginary Grudges, Relationships or Vain-glory.
7 **Divisions**, 1, The Temptation;
    2, Finding the Lost Master-word;
    3, Murder and Baptism.

Minor Points

1 **Element**, Air.
2 **Sign**, Virgo, or the Liver and Vitals.
3 **Sign-parts**, Pegasus, Branch and Centaur.
4 **Planet**, The Sun as seen from the Earth.
5 **Color**, Orange.
6 **Greek Philosopher**, Socrates.
7 **Hindu Philosopher**, Vaiseshika.
8 **Ethnic Religion**, The Druids.

SEVENTH DEGREE

The Griffin, — Reincarnation.

(A shallow cave, rocky, with two small grottoes on either hand, lit with dim colored lights. The back-ground is formed by two large gates now closed behind which lies a deeper mystery cave. It is night, and cold. Sitting around a smouldering heap of fire-wood, the *Initiates* shiver and yawn,)

1, **The** Temptation.

Camillus, This cave will shelter us to-night, at least.
Mysta, Meseems it is not the time for idle speech.
(*Camillus* investigates the caves, but is drawn back by *Mysta,* who betrays anxiety, and says,)
Mysta, No separations till the morning light!
Camillus, Then I was not the only one who saw somewhat?
  What saw you in the cloud upon the Bridge?
Mysta, How strange what different ghosts beset our path!
Camillus, I'll guard, in case that Terror here pursues.
  Mutual confession would relieve our doubts.
Mysta, I hardly dare to speak of what I saw.
  A Shape of Gloom approached, and said to me,
  'In spite of all this solemn Judgment-scene,
  What if your Judges were less just than you?
  God may be just in heaven, where there is naught
    To overcome; but what of invalids?

Camillus, And what of babes that die in infancy?

Mysta, What of the men born saints, and sinners born?
What of the insane, or idiots from their birth?

Camillus, Civilization is the lot of some,
    Others born Bushmen, Helots, Hottentots.

Mysta, What of the double standard; is that just?

Camillus, Not unto every race have saviors come.

Mysta, Should those who love be sundered evermore?

Camillus, There is no God for slaves on auction block.

Mysta, Poverty brutalizes children who
    In childhood showed ability and grace. -

Camillus, And then the accidents, misfortunes, and
    Ironies of our fate, that have inspired
      The proverb, 'Those whom the Gods have loved
                          die young.'
    God is not just!

Mysta,   I think we better pray! (Silence).

(Apparently as answer to this the *Herald* blows a solemn slow blast. The gates open, emitting a great light. Vested in light brown, enter the)

Magus, After the storm, welcome unto this Cave!
    Welcome you are, but welcome unto work.
    Because of accident, we will admit
    To-morrow noon those who before that time
    Discovered treasure hidden in this Cave.

Maga, Who shall not find shall be refused more light;
    And for one year must roam around these rocks.
    Wherefore I say, 'You *must,* you *shall* succeed!'
    Farewell, my Children, till the hour of noon!

(They turn to go, but *Camillus* shamefacedly pulls their cloak to retain them.)

Camillus, Father, forgive us; but we are at fault.
    The Fiends that stood beside the Judgment Bridge

Smote us so sore we do not even wish
To seek the treasure that you bid us find,
Until our awful doubts may be resolved.

Mysta, From things we know we doubt that God is just.

Maga, And what, my Children, do you think you know?

Camillus, God is not just to slaves, to women weak,
The poor, the pagan, aborigines;
Misfortunes chiefly happen to the good.

Magus, (To blushing MYSTA,) And what have you to say?

Mysta, God is not just to early-dying babes;
To invalids, to saints or sinners born,
To idiots or insane, in accidents,
To lovers sundered by disease or death.

Camillus, (to Mages,) O Wise and Strong, who have our confidence,
Merely assure our souls that God is just,
As you direct, we will proceed on faith!

Mages, What you have said we cannot contradict.
(The *Candidates* in consternation; whispers from)

Camillus, Then I was right that we have been misled?

Maga, Not so, my son; I keep my peace because
I am unwilling to defraud your soul
Of blessing, as hereafter shall appear.

Magus, This much I'll say: Your doubts are not original;
All Candidates who mastered this Degree
Have had to solve them, and were satisfied.
So, we repeat, discover hidden pelf.

Maga, Children, reflect; have we e'er played you false?
Further obedience, more enlightenment, —

SEVENTH, the GRIFFIN

Not from without, but from within yourself.

Mystics, (doggedly), We will obey, although it be with tears.

Mages, Also with tears, farewell; also with prayers!

(After they have gone, the *Mystics* look at each other, sit down pray silently and weep. Finally *Camillus* picks up the spades left by the *Mages*,)

Camillus, Sister, you take the grotto on the left,
While I shall labor on the right hand cell;
Whoever first succeeds shall cry aloud.

(They work in the soft sand, and find only small square stone blocks, which they discard contemptuously. In despair they return to their respective seats. A gong sounds; gestures and words of indignation at the shortness of the time. A *Herald* comes out from the Gate, closes the door behind him, and genially asks,)

Herald, Which one of you may I congratulate?

Camillus, Neither; in treasure-trove we disbelieve.

Herald, (gently), Now was your search entirely in vain?
Only last night that treasure was put there.

Camillus, Pebbles were all that she or I could find.

Herald, Then bring the pebbles; precious they may prove;
If they are what you find, it must be they.
Hasten, because an accident occurred.

2, Finding of the Lost Master-word.

(A gong sounds, as an alarm; cries of 'Murder! Help! Catch the murderers!' Roughly the doors are drawn back, revealing the *Mages* lying prostrate before their altar, on which stands the image of a griffin [the body of a lion with an eagle's head] from the eyes, nose and mouth of which issues the only illumination. *Priests*, garbed as *Fiends*, armed with swords and spears, which they brandish, cry loud and confusedly. The *Arch-Fiend* stands between the corpses, and accusingly points to the *Mystics'* gloved hands whose gloves, in the new light, are revealed as being bloody, to the *Mystics'* surprised confusion.)

SEVENTH, *the GRIFFIN*

Fiend, Deny the murder, O you parricides!
    You criminals, monsters in human form!
    As test of guilt, I shall administer
    The murderer's oath; down on your knees!

(*Camillus*'s hands are placed on the *Mages*' heads; those of *Mysta,* on their hearts. The *Mystics*' hands, being bloody, stick to the *Mages*' bodies. *Fiends* hold daggers to the *Mystics*' throats.)

Fiend, As you will feel, the Mages' bodies are
    Not yet entirely frigid, not yet stiff.
    As soon as they are so, you both shall die.
    If on the contrary you can restore
    Them unto life, you both shall be released;
    So hasten, ere their flames of life be quenched!

Camillus, Oh that I knew what could restore to life!

Fiend, Since by a word God has created worlds,
    Why not try on them the lost Master-word?

Mysta, How should we use it, if it has been lost?

Fiend, Have you not found somewhat?

Camillus, Nothing but stones.

Fiend, Then must those stones contain the word you
                                  seek.
    Examine them!

(Roughly the *Fiends* throw on the ground the stones that had been discovered, and drive the *Mystics* to examine them.)

Camillus, Miracle! mine bear letters!

Mysta,   So do mine!

Fiend, And what do letters form, if not some word?

(Feverishly shuffling them, and uttering a cry of discovery,)

Camillus, They form the word *Civilization!*

(*Magus* stirs, opens his eyes, groans, and slowly begins to rise.)

Camillus, Discovered is the Master-word at last!
    Released from guilt, and also freed from doubt!

Fiend, But save the MAGA, MYSTA, or you die!

(In desperation, *Mysta* shrieks *Civilization!* into both ears of *Maga,* but without the slightest beneficial effect.)

Mysta, God help me, for I know not what to do!

Magus, MYSTA, have you no other Master-word?

Mysta, So there could be more master-words than one?

Magus, Of course, each human soul lives off its own;
    Discover yours, before it be too late!

(*Mysta* shuffles her pebbles, suddenly she cries,)

Mysta, I have it, quick! *Reincarnation!*

(As she shouts in *Maga's* ears, the latter moves and wakes.)

Maga, MYSTA, yourself your doubts you have resolved
    For all your puzzles would have disappeared
    Had there been lives, before or after, which
    Could justify the injustices you felt,

Magus, While progress of Civilization
    Will solve the problems MYSTUS here had felt.

Maga, So now your puzzles you yourselves have cleared,

Magus, While we in death objectively explained
    The realms that complement this troubled life;
    Now must you see how souls reenter it.

3, Reincarnation of the Soul.

(*Attendants* throw over the shoulders of the *Initiates* light brown robes, and place on their heads lofty turbans. A little *Baby* is brought in.)

Maga, Behold the infant born into the world,
    And you who represent the Powers of Birth
    Shall introduce the SEVEN PRINCIPLES

(The officiators act out the words,)

SEVENTH, *the GRIFFIN*

Magus, The mystic gates of body are the pores,
  We smear them with red earth in sign of birth.
Mystics, Glory to God for the power of thought and the working of wisdom,
  Glory for ever and ever, Amen.
Maga, The navel was the finer body's gate;
  With orange oil its seat we consecrate.
Mystics, Glory to God for his help in attainment of righteousness,
  Glory for ever and ever, Amen.
Magus, The mouth is gate of the vitality,
  Which yellow water thus will symbolize.
Mystics, Glory to God for the strength of our lives, and our hope of attaining immortality,
  Glory for ever and ever, Amen.
Maga, The ear admits the soul intuitive,
  Which greenish salt will fitly represent.
Mystics, Glory to God who in love never wearies in justice,
  Glory for ever and ever, Amen.
Magus, Synthetic knowledge operates through eyes,
  Which is by topaz alcohol explained.
Mystics, Glory to God in the name of his Angel-redeemers,
  Glory for ever and ever, Amen.
Maga, Blue ether fumes through nostrils operate,
  As spiritual soul from God descends.
Mystics, Glory to God, the Father of Spirits and Ruler of Angels,
  Glory for ever and ever, Amen.
Magus, On forehead's wrinkles violet shades I bow,
  As spiritual influences breathe.
Mystics, Glory to God the Triune, the Supreme and Immortal,
  Glory for ever and ever, Amen.

Magus, Let us pray, I will declare a secret to the Initiated, but let the doors be wholly shut against the Profane! Suffer not the prepossession of your mind to deprive you of that happy life which the knowledge of those mysterious truths will procure you. Yes, look at the Divine Nature! Incessantly contemplate it, and govern well the mind and heart so as to keep on progressing towards vision of the sole Governor of the Universe. He is the Fusion of Power, Knowledge and Love into Wisdom. Just as He is the Source whence all things derive, so does He operate through all, though never seen by mortal eyes, though Himself seen by none, yet Himself seeing all. The soul comes from everlasting, and goes to Final Fruition; being seen and acting only in the Flash of Transition. The God of Justice be praised! Amen, Amen, and Amen!

4, Initiation.

Herald, (trumpets and cries,) Down on your knees by the steps! (*Mystics* obey and raise their hands,)

Mystics, We swear to trust in the Justice of God;
But as its purpose were defeated by
Publicity, so we will not divulge
The details of transition of the Soul;
But the distressed we promise to console.

Mysta, I will explain the inequalities
Of Nature, by Reincarnation's law.

Camillus, I will abate injustices of life
By speeding up Civilization's growth.

(*Attendants* cover them with a griffin's eagle head-mask, and with robes resembling a lion's mane and tail, all smeared with blood.)

SEVENTH, *the* GRIFFIN

Magus, No longer Ravens, sacred Griffins, rise,
   Showing the amphibiousness of the human soul;
   They err that think that this one life is all!
   An eagle out of lion's life may grow;
   Each one of you some former animal,
   Now lion grown, and eagle soon to be,
   A lower past, with future prophecy.
   To higher eyes you also griffins seem,
   An animal at heart, with head of bird;
   Creeping on earth, with an aspiring glance,
   Not yet evolved from passions leonine,
   Already uttering cries of upper air.

Camillus, What mean these blood-dyed robes?
Magus,   The savior's robe!
   A deed of selflessness makes man a priest,
   As woman is made priest by child-bed blood;
   For in a world in which there is a mother-love
   There also is vicarious sacrifice
   For the emergencies, the sudden chance.
   Perhaps, for the nonce, a bandage will hold
   The rich red blood of some heroic heart;
   A single touch may save a climber's life.

Maga, Wherefore, beside Reincarnation's law,
   To speed it, rather, initiates must help
   The ignorant and suffering world;
   Must our civilization's progress speed,
   In course of which you surely bleed and die.
   Just as it was worth while for us to die,
   Murdered by you, to let you steal from us
   The Master-word that destiny unlocks.

Magus, Like us, as teachers shall you wear these robes
   Ready for slaughter by the souls you feed;
   With revelation of the Master-word
   Of Reincarnation, that consoles and nerves;
   But when you meet a Rabbin, you shall die!

5, Revelation of the Messiah.

Camillus, Was our baptizing of that little babe
    Only to learn how souls reincarnate?
Maga. Kneel down, while I the mystery reveal!
(They kneel, each putting one hand on the Babe on the altar.)
Maga, Scan well his face; will you remember it?
Mystics, We will!
Maga, This child is the Messiah of your age;
    Each one someday shall meet him on his path;
    And if you recognize him, will receive
    His benediction, if you still hold fast
    Your life-long mission of apostolate.
    He has no name, so that whoever comes
    To you as if from him, he is a fraud.
Mysta, How could we know him then?
Magus,   Not by himself,
    But by the words he speaks, his miracles.
    Like Magi from the East, all your life long,
    With tear-myrrh, deed-gold, prayer-frankincense,
    Forsaking home, through deserts should you fare,
    In search of where this Babe shall be reborn,
    Catching a glimpse of his impassive eyes;
    That is the worship that he asks of you.
Maga, He will await you by Death's icy stream
    And guide your steps unto a Dwelling New;
    And by the knowledge that you here have gained
    You will know how to capture some new form
    In which To-day's ideals will come true:
    Your own apostles, and your masters own!
(The light has faded, the altar has sunk down; the *Mages*, carrying the *Baby*, disappear by a back door.)
Magus, Farewell, O sacred Griffins!
Maga,   Till we meet
    Upon some other shore, in better time!

Questions to be Answered in Writing 🖉 7

Not to be answered all at once, but each on the indicated day of the month, overlapping from 22nd to 22nd.

The ideal time to study this Degree alone is in Aug to Sept'ber If the whole series is to be taken, it is best to begin on Oct 22.

But the first 22nd after you hear of these Degrees is the time Providence has set for *your* beginning; *anything* ranks delay.

Day 22, Read and copy the Degree, and memorize your favorite selections therefrom, and record them.

Day 23, Mention the 12 chief *Injustices of Life.*

Day 24, To gloss over a misfortune (leaving it as a possible danger-point of trouble and suspicion,) or to face it bravely (rendering it harmless by intelligent cure,) — which is the better way, and how does it appear in this degree?

Day 25, What is the sole object of obedience to divine precepts, injunctions and laws?

Day 26, What is the significance of the murder-scene?

Day 27, Why and how does a master-word restore to life?

Day 28, How many master-words are there?

Day 29, Which six life-injustices are explained away by which master-word?

Day 30, Which other six are explained away by which other one?

Day 1, Which principle is necessary to fructify and complete reincarnation?

Day 2, What is the significance of the baptism-scene?

Day 3, Mention the human body's seven gates, and which soul-parts enter through which?

Day 4, Memorize and reproduce the *Gloria.*

Practical Experiments to be Reported 7

Day 5, Every evening go over the events of the day, backwards and then forwards. The immediate object of this is to act as a daily self-judgment of the soul, and includes keeping a diary; it was recommended by Pythagoras.

Day 6, Its more occult purpose, however, is to act as first step towards *continued consciousness*, (i.e. bridging the gap of sleep.) Extend the reviewing habit gradually until you devote every Saturday evening to a *mental* review of the past week. Written records should be kept, but should usurp the *primary* achievement of mental power.

Day 7, Extend the practise to 30 days, devoting the 22nd of every month to this *mensiversary*.

Day 8, Extend this practise to the *anniversary* of your birth, which is really the *council of your gods*.

Day 9, Extend this practise to seven years, constituting one of the 7 Shakesperian ages of your life.

Day 10, It will now be evident that this practise is the basis of successful reincarnation. Read Walker *Reincarnation*; Johnston, *Memory of Past Births*.

Day 11, Record your memories from past existences.

Day 12, Record your experiences that something similar has happened before.

Day 13, Gather and examine your most persistent dreams.

Day 14, Examine them in the light of memories.

Day 15, Daily allow your fancy free rein in inventing a past existence, down to minutest details.

Day 16, Record these systematically up to 1000.

Day 17, Examine these for persistence, veridicalness.

Day 18, List and avoid possible (Theosophical) misuse of Reincarnation. List its possibilities for good.

EIGHTH DEGREE

The Persian Hero

Calling of the Saviors.

The Mithraic Mysteries, Modernized.

Eighth Degree, the Hero.

Major Points

1 **Symbol**, Perseus, or the Hero.
2 **Purpose**, Redemptive service.
3 **Scene**, The Telestic Cave, where initiates are led to the Altar over what seems to be an Abyss.
4 **Peculiarity**, Calls for help from Beggars who were really Messengers summoning to Initiation.
5 **Temptation**, To refuse help to the Needy.
6 **Oath**, To seek the Master-Word, revealed by Social Service.
7 **Divisions**, 1, Home Heroism; 2 Calling of the Saviors; 3 Initiation. 4 Instruction 5 Communion 6 Farewells.

Minor Points

1 **Element**, Air.
2 **Sign**, Leo, or the Heart.
3 **Sign-parts**, Lynx, Hydra and Leo Minor.
4 **Planet**, The Planetoids, and the Lost Planet.
5 **Color**, Green.
6 **Greek Philosopher**, Plato.
7 **Hindu Philosopher**, Nyaya.
8 **Ethnic Religion**, The Norse Edda.

EIGHTH DEGREE

The Persian Hero — Call to Saviorship

1, Introduction

(The same rocky cave, There is a good fire burning in the centre, with the remains of a meagre supper.)

Camillus, O Mysta, sing again!

Mysta, What shall I sing?
   Gladly I will, if you will give a theme;
   I have run out entirely my store
   Of memories my mother taught to me.

Camillus, Most beautiful it was, that lovely tale
   How dying Mary her beloved consoled
   Revealing how Reincarnation saved!
   Happy it made these months. What is its name?

Mysta, 'Tis called the REUNITING PILGRIMAGE.

Camillus, And did your mother write it?

Mysta, No indeed.
   By chance she found an ancient Christian roll
   Writ by the Gnostic sage BASILIDES
   Who claimed it was a SECOND BOOK OF ACTS.
   With it she whiled away our evenings long.

Camillus, But you must have prodigious memory
   To have recalled that epic lay entire.

Mysta, It was not memory; I had forgotten it.

Camillus, Then how could you recite it perfectly?

Mysta, It was not memory at all; I felt

        My mother's smiling spirit standing near,
        Seeming to put the words into my mouth.

Camillus, Reincarnation then was old to you,
        This initiation then was but a farce?

Mysta, No, not a farce; I had forgotten all
        My childhood's dreams; and in maturer years
        Needed a surer philosophic grasp,
        And recollection. Was not PLATO right
        That initiation reminiscence is?

Camillus, Yes, we were originally divine. —
        But now can you remember something more?

Mysta, Weary I feel; and I have done my share.
        Can n't you contribute entertainment too?

Camillus, I will propose, for crown of heroism
        During the sixty days we here have spent,
        Her who performed the little home-like deeds,
        The fire, the water, and the little chores,
        The food, the stitches and the midnight watch;
As you have watched, may angels watch o'er you!
        Here is a chaplet which I offer her,
        Proclaiming her the Queen of this our cave.

Mysta, Quite so; but first of my high royal acts
        Shall be to crown as consort to my throne
        Him who has cut and gathered fire-wood,
        Whose intuition warned of all mischance,
        Whose judgment solved the problems that arose,
        Who killed intruding vermin, cleaned the hall,
        Provided food, and crystal water brought.
        As I descend, so rise, King our Cave!

Camillus, What I accept is only for the Lord,
        The blest inspirer of our holiness!

Mysta, To him who lives as vicar of the Lord
        Shall come all honors of their own accord.

EIGHTH, *the* PERSIAN HERO

2, *The* Calling *of the* Saviors.

(While they are still waving their chaplets, from the distance they hear a man rushing up the rocks, try to enter the cave, and cry, *Help! Saviors, help! Hell has broken loose!* The *Mystics* erect a barrier at the gate.)

Mysta, Stop, perhaps the man has genuine need.

Camillus, Your heart has weakened?

Mysta, Let me look and see!
(Bandaging her eyes and ears,)

Camillus, You shall be saved, e'en in your own despite!

Mysta, Perhaps I shall be spared, but not this way,
  For thus my inner vision is more clear!
I will describe the man; he wears a Hebrew cap,..

Camillus, (looking discouraged), She is right! I might as well release her sight.

Mysta, Oh no, clearer I see! Emergencies
  Demand a clearer knowledge of God's will.

Hebrew, (outside) O Saviors, help us! Hell has broken loose;
  The Dragon whom great Michael dispossessed
  Of heavenly fields, because he grew so proud
  As to suppose himself like unto God,
  Cast upon earth, and falling into hell,
  In Tophet burning with the flames of Sheol,
  Demands another Michael to save,
  Or all the earth shall perish in a day.
  Help, O you Good Ones on the Mountain here!

Camillus, My friend, we here are waiting other things;
  We are awaiting deeper Mysteries.

Hebrew, And meanwhile let good men die off?

Camillus, You speak as if we had the strength you need

Hebrew, Then why at least not do the best you can?
Camillus, We have been told to wait the next Degree
Hebrew, Than saving lives there's no Degree more high.
Camillus, Oh that our initiators would direct!
Hebrew, What need of them when needs come up to you?
Camillus, How do we know that you are not a trap?
Hebrew, Poor gods who have not intuition learned!
Camillus, Gods will avenge insults to oracles.
Hebrew, The only oracle I want is help.
Mysta, That oracle I hear within myself;
   I'll go with you and do the best I can!
Camillus, You shall not go; your going I forbid!
Hebrew, What mean these barricades, and such command
   Within this Cave of Mysteries and Truth?
   That girl is mine; unless at once she come
   I will break down the door, fetch her myself!
Camillus, I dare you to!

(The *Hebrew* does so, and seizes *Mysta,* who runs towards him but then turns towards *Camillus* and cries to him,)

Mysta, Fear not, CAMILLUS, for I well can see
   An angel shining through this outside rough.
Hebrew, (gently), And where, my valiant warrior, is your sword?

(*Mysta* takes her seven-runged ladder that had served her to climb into the grotto,)

Mysta, It is all I have; I will carry it with me!
Hebrew, It is all you will need, my Child! Be not afraid!
   Call out farewell, and make the coward cry!

EIGHTH, *the* PERSIAN HERO

Mysta, Comrade, farewell! Be of good cheer because...
(The *Hebrew* drags her off before she can complete her sentence.)
Camillus, And this is then the end of all our hopes?
    We who had hoped to see blest Mithra's face,
    Lost! Gone! — Our initiators are to blame;
    How could we know how to detect the false?
    Lest further evil should arise, thereby
    Stopping the initiations, I will hide;
    And vain shall be the coming Devil's search!

(He tries to hide in his grotto; but out from it comes a blind *Greek Girl* groping and crying.)
Greek Girl, Help me, O PERSEUS, come and save my land!
    Andromeda my play-mate is chained to rocks
    Until the Dragon come and drag her off!
    Queen Cassiopœa boasted that she was
    More handsome e'en than Juno; so the god
    Of Ocean, Neptune, harried all our land,
    And none can free king Cepheus' realm, or her,
    But you, O PERSEUS, whom the oracle
    Of Ammon, and all Joppa hereby calls!
Camillus, I am not PERSEUS, just a neophyte.
Greek Girl, That is the same to me; just come and save,
    And call yourself whatever name you please!
Camillus, But Ammon's oracle demanded him!
Greek Girl, For him no more I ask; I ask for you!
    Strong in my weakness, in my blindness keen,
    On Judgment Day with scorn I'll point at you
Unless you, you whom I touch, come with me!
(Out of pity, he had approached to soothe her. But she lays hold of him, though he recoils in terror.)
Camillus, Caught! Caught in a trap! Also I am lost!

I hate you, girl! I will go on with you,
But do not dare to speak another word!
Betrayed! Give me my ladder! I will fight!
Also be blinded! For myself I weep!
I who have worked so long to scale the heavens
Lost in the quicksands of adventures wild!
And so these initiations are at end!
The MAGES have neglected us too long!
They are to blame, — our duty is to save.

3, The Initiation.

(The doors open and reveal the altar surrounded by the *Mages* and the priests. On either side a pedestal, about three feet from the walls, opposite to which, in the rock-walls, are trap-doors, about one foot above the ground, with pans of water between them and the pedestals. In the sanctuary *Attendants* are making fierce noises as of lions, dragons and wild beasts. The *Mystics*, garbed to represent *Michael* and *Perseus*, and blind-folded, are introduced through the trap-doors, one from each side. They are struggling with the *Guides* who are introducing them,)

Camillus, Why was I blind-folded, if my aid was sought?

Guide, To save you natural but needless fear
   Till close the horrid beast you are to kill,
   And which you now so very plainly hear.

Mysta, I feel the road has stopped! My foot has slipped
   Into a rushing river! Treachery! Help!

Guide, Can you not save yourself?

Mysta,   My ladder's length
   Is far too short.

Guide,   Try it!

Mysta,   It reaches ground;
   But I might fall!

EIGHTH, *the PERSIAN HERO*

Guide, God's angels would support!
    (*Mysta* rushes across, stumbles, but is saved.)
Camillus, Such rash experiment I will refuse;
    I stay, and will return unto the Mystic Cave!
Guide, You shall return, but over the abyss!

(The *Guide* beats *Camillus* with a whip until the latter, in self-defense, rushes across. Then *Attendants* lead the *Mystics* onto the pedestals, whispering to them that all is well, and removing their blinders, which however makes no difference, as all is dark. The *Attendants* then say farewell, and descend the pedestals' seven steps. While the beasts' roarings proceed there is heard the rough loud crying of a)

Herald, Savior of man, before you dare your deed,
    To God yourself commend, and swear the oath
    If you should be victorious, nevermore
    To man reveal the Terror you have met, —
    A miracle alone can save you here,—
Who would have light must raise his hand and swear
Mystics, We do.
(Light floods the scene, revealing the *Mages* by their altars.)

Mages, Blessed be Michael purifying heaven!
    Blessed be Perseus, rescuing the lost!

Chorus, Unto the awful overpowering spirits of the
                                       Faithful
    Unto the spirits of those who taught the essentials
                                        of the Faith,
    Be blessing and honor for ever and ever, Amen!
Through their brightness and glory the sky shines afar,
    Looking like a palace of celestial substance,
Looking as if God was wearing a robe inlaid with stars.
It is through the saints' brightness and glory that child-
                                       ren in the womb develop,
    Each miraculous part achieving its due proportion.

The most powerful spirits are those that taught the Law
    In its pristine purity and simplicity.
Next to them are the spirits of those who shall guard
    Benevolent souls at the Restoration of the World.
He who travels roads dangerous, fearful and awesome
    Might well contemplate, praise and invoke the Unseen Helpers,
Who heal the sick, and enhalo those who pray.
Keenest of urgers, slowest retirers, who never turn their backs,
    Safest of bridges, truest aimed of weapons,
    They sit in silence, gazing inquisitorially,
    As if a thousand men were watching over that soul;
    Their friendship lasts long, they are never the first to do harm,
    The greater the need, the closer they come,
    As birds flying, but with the wings of love.
We worship the Saints' intellect, perception and conscience,
We worship the Helpers of the Latter Days' restoration,
We worship the souls of the holy men and women
    Born at any time, present, past or future,
    Whose consciences direct, or whose will struggles,
    Or have ever struggled for the good!

4, The Instruction.

Magus, We watched your drama of conferring crowns
    And when you thought yourselves the most alone,
    Nearest were we, and sent those calls for help.
Maga, Nor were you left alone, except to help
    You gain your saviorship, impossible
    While you relied on us, had we been near.

EIGHTH, the PERSIAN HERO

Magus, The dragons whtch you were called out to fight
    Was shrinking cowardice within yourselves.

Maga, These ladders which as weapons you assumed
    Were seven-runged, betokening your souls:
    Former Degrees are weapons saviors need;
    And more, is all that you can use,
    Material weapons being trumpery.

Magus, But little did you think, when calls came up,
    That you were shaping your own destiny.
    That choice, too serious for the spheral gods,
    Was thus remanded into your own hands, —
    Judge of the value of the little deed!
    Yourselves decided whither you should fare;
And more, which deaths each one of you should die,
What converts make, what lessons you should learn,
    And at what heaven each at last arrive.
    Yet, spite of your responsibility,
    The song of destiny you have but sung.
    This is the Tower of Babel: each his choice;
    Well may you weep, already far apart!

Maga, This is the teaching of the Eighth Degree:
    Who loses his own self redeems his soul.
    Had you remained out there, you had been lost.

Magus, By sacrifice you have true PERSIANS grown;
    Kneel down, receive the Persian's great reward:
    'The soul that saves the world shall save itself,
    Make Heaven more fair, and more divine the gods!'

Maga, Upon this altar see this sacrament
    As universal as its many names:
    Nectar, ambrosia, Scaldic mead, or Grail,
    Hindu amritsa, shew-bread of the Jews,
    The cruse and barrel of Zarephath's home,
    The desert-manna falling every morn.

Come and partake of immortality
To give your spirit strength to carry out
The missions which yourselves dared undertake,
Which are impossible sans miracle,
For which, as for all else, you need your God.

(Then the *Persii* are communicated by anointing with milk and honey on the forehead, ear and nose, and by being given a leaf containing some honey to eat. Palms from the altar are given to each of the *Mystics*. Then the lights suddenly go out, obliterating everything except the haloes of the *Mystics* and *Mages*. Between them however rises a shaft of greenish light, and there booms forth a sepulchral)

Voice, In those far latter days of aging earth
When stars and moon and winds and tides shall fail,
    A savior shall arise, called SAYOSHANT,
    To shepherd souls for immortality.
    This is the secret of the Phœnix tale,
    Which from its ashes young again arose,
    Thrilling with currents of diviner life;
    So go and preach the Phœnix to the world!

(The column of light is dimned; tongues of flame descend upon the *Neophytes*; their heads shine.)

Magus, Let lights be made! [They are made.]
Maga, Children, declare the vision you have seen.
    So what saw Michael?
Mysta,   Three crosses on a hill!
Maga, And Perseus?
Camillus,   A lyre and a harp;
    A mountain which is the abode of song,
    A rainbow over it, with lake of light
    Reflecting it, until the whole was fire: —
    Behold, I think that I have seen the Lord!

EIGHTH, *the PERSIAN HERO*

4, *The* Farewells.

Magus, Persians and heroes, this the hour supreme!
    This Degree's Master-word must now be given;
    Are you both ready for the last attempt?

Mystics, [low and sadly,] We are! [Lights go out.]

Maga, The Master-word is never given out
    And never must by you be e'en pronounced
    Except in darkness such as now you feel,
    Which is the terror of Medusa's head;
    Except while bending down upon one knee,
    As kneeled Andromeda upon the rock;
    Except the right hand to the forehead held,
    The left extended towards the unseen sun,
    As Perseus held the Gorgon on his shield.

Mystics, We swear.

Magus, Children, the Master-word is never *given;*
    It is *received* from heaven whence Perseus came;
    Wherefore you must go forth, nor cease till found;
As Argonauts fare forth to fetch the Golden Fleece!
    When here we meet next month, if all agree,
    You will be sure that none has been deceived!

Mystics, We go!

Camillus, But tell us, MAGES, why it must be hid
    In starless gloom, and kneeling on one knee,
    With right to brow, and left extended forth?

Magus, For prayer's true posture helps in time of need
    Only to prayer the Word shall be revealed.

Mysta, What weapon shall we take upon our quest?

Maga, Your ladders will be bridges, staves and beds.
    As substitute for magic word, their name
    Is PERSEUS, which in trouble used, will call
    Great hosts of angels, from the seven realms,
Who unseen will flock round and bring God's help.

138 EIGHTH, the PERSIAN HERO

Camillus, What is the magic of the PERSIAN name?
Magus, Each of the seven letters means one realm
    Of seven-fold soul: physical body and
    Etheric body; reproduction, soul,
    Intellect, understanding, spirit last.
    Uniting these initials forms a name,
    Which means that when the planes together act
    Results a man, a savior and a god.
Maga, All this is wisdom, perfectly expressed,
    But be you sure you use it perfectly!
    So now farewell! And choose your way between
    The ivory door of dreams, and grief's horn door.
Magus, Now choose according to the vision seen;
    Each is predestined by his symbol's gleam.
    Who saw three crosses on a hill?
Mysta, It was I, the Persius MICHAEL!
(*Maga* opens the right hand door with a crash; out from it comes sulphurous smoke, and a terrible voice, *Eli, Eli, lama sabachthani?*)
Maga, There lies your road, my child!
All,   Farewell!
Maga, My Child, there are three steps that lead up there
    No more can you here tell the colors than
    Most men distinguish bodies from their souls,
    And both from spirit, that are sundered here.
(*Mysta* ascends more carefully, feeling her way with her ladder. The awful *Voice* speaks again. She cries, *Farewell!* Other voices answer, *Farewell! God help you!* A gong clangs eleven. The others are heard praying and cheering, *Persius!* The same action for *Camillus.*)
Maga, Who saw a lyre and harp?
Camillus, It was I, the Persius PERSEUS!
(*Magus* opens the left-hand door. A terrible agonized *Voice* cries *Eurydice is gone!* Sulphurous fumes, smoke, curses, howling, *Abomination of the earth!*)
Magus, This is your road, my Son; watch for the steps!
Camillus, MYSTA is gone, so, all of you, farewell!
        (Door bangs to; gong clangs twelve.)
Magus, And will they both return?
Maga,   God only knows!

Questions to be Answered in Writing 🖉 8

Not to be answered all at once, but each on the indicated
day of the month, overlapping from 22nd to 22nd.

The ideal time to study this Degree alone is in July to August.
If the whole series is to be taken, it is best to begin on Nov. 22.
But the first 22nd after you hear of these Degrees is the time
Providence has set for *your* beginning; *anything* ranks delay.

DAY 22, Read and copy the Degree, and memorize your favorite selections therefrom, and record them.

Day 23, Who is the likeliest to enter heaven?

Day 24, That a call to help someone is in reality an opportunity for improvement, illustrate from the Degree, and then from contemporary history.

Day 25, Why is it useless to blind our external eyes to applicants for help?

Day 26, If forced to choose between an opportunity for initiation and a *definite call* for help, which should you follow? Illustrate from the Degree, and from a famous American poem, which learn.

Day 27, What is the significance of the Ladder?

Day 28, Deep abysses yawn around our path of life; what are they in reality?

Day 29, What is the only weapon that is efficient?

Day 30, What were the neophytes who chose the calls for help really doing?

Day 1, What is the spiritual significance of the legend of the Phœnix?

Day 2, What is the spiritual significance of being a *Persian*, and how is it achieved?

Day 3, What is the posture in which alone the oath should be taken? What does it mean?

Day 4, Mention the legends connected with each of the saviors mentioned.

Practical Experiments to be Reported 🕮 8

Day 5, Gather many quotations agreeing with the text, *He that loseth his life shall find it.*

Day 6, List famous heroes who did so.

Day 7, Do some such unselfish deed.

Day 8, Observe and record the curious and otherwise unexplainable interior satisfaction, transcending that derived from any selfish pleasure.

Day 9, Try to identify, and then examine each of the seven parts of your soul, giving each a percentage rating for order, efficiency and ability.

Day 10, Work at their deficiencies, so as to allow each a daily expression sufficient to improve each into a symmetrical part of a symmetrical whole which is developing towards a divine destiny.

Day 11, Gather a club of children, take them on an excursion, teach a Sunday School class, or perform some other social service deed.

Day 12, Observe and record the interior result.

Day 13, List the social service activities of your town, and discover some as yet unexercised field.

Day 14, Accomplish some creative religious work in that direction.

Day 15, Do one each of the following: give alms, console the sorrowing, visit a hospital, prison or penitentiary, and relieve the need of some self-respecting person, who would be the last one to ask for help.

Day 16, List and compare the resulting interior experiences, which are a divine witness.

Day 17, Learn to recognize unintentional signals of distress.

Day 18, Relieve these, in an impersonal way, if possible.

NINTH DEGREE

The Scarabaeus

Building of Sanctuaries.

The Mithraic Mysteries, Modernized.

Ninth Degree, the Scarabaeus.

Major Points

1 **Symbol**, Scarabæus, or the Sacred Beetle.
2 **Purpose**, Planning Noble Dreams.
3 **Scene**, The Telestic Cave, where are built small shrines of different racial architectures.
4 **Peculiarity**, They must be built in absolute silence.
5 **Temptation**, To remain in the old sanctuaries.
6 **Oath**, Not to reveal the plans on their charts, because they are individual.
7 **Divisions**, 1, Introduction, Building.
    2, Consecration of the Shrines.
    3, Instruction, and leaving of the Shrines.

Minor Points

1 **Element**, Air.
2 **Sign**, Cancer, or the Chest.
3 **Sign-parts**, Sagitta, Lyra and Ursa Minor.
4 **Planet**, Uranus.
5 **Color**, Purple.
6 **Greek Philosopher**, Aristotle.
7 **Hindu Philosopher**, Shankya.
8 **Ethnic Religion**, American Mysteries: the White Ant, the Bird of Paradise.

The Ninth Degree

The Scarabœus, — Sanctuary-Building

(The same cave, the *Mages* sitting on rocks at the entrance, shading their eyes, looking for the *Mystics*.)

Magus, How long it seems since both the children went!
Maga, I wonder if indeed they will return?
Magus, I hear them; quick, let us return within!

(They reenter by the right side door. Enter *Camillus*, dragging himself in, his robe stained and bloody. He looks around seeming to seek *Mysta*. Suddenly he runs out and returns with her,)

Camillus, To see you safe is more than I had hoped!
So hard were the experiences I had!
Mysta, They will appear more sweet in retrospect,
Transfigured by the victory we won!

(The left wicket opens, *Priests* come out.)

Herald, The Hierophants command your eyes be bound
And you be led into the Sanctuary.
But you will be refused without the WORD
Last month you went to seek, and find and learn.
Mysta, I cannot give it but in darkness deep,
The knee to ground, right hand to brow, left stretched.

(The stage grows dark. The *Mystics* assume that position, and cry *Phœnix!* The light returns, and the *Priests* congratulate them. They are admitted as soon as the central doors, which are yellow in color, and show scarabæi, are opened. At the altar the *Mystics* allow their eyes to be bound, and they kneel.)

Mages, Swear that you will never betray the sight
    That unto you at present we reveal.

Mystics,   We swear!

(The bandages are removed, and they see two black charts showing white pictures of small kiosks, in Hebrew and Persian temple-styles.)

Magus, These are such charts as the initiate PAUL
    In Seventh Heaven beheld upon the Mount
    As pattern of the Temple to be built;
    And MOSES saw on Sinai to plan
    The Tabernacle for the Israelites.
    So here you see the patterns of your shrines
    That you yourselves must build ere you attain.

Maga, Of course those buildings are symbolic of
  The differing trainings you have given your souls:
    Each thought a stone, and *As you live you build.*

Magus, Engrave these upon the tablets of your hearts;
    Should you forget, your temples would remain
    Imperfect, incomplete forevermore,
    And all the world be poorer by your loss.

Maga, The sole condition of your building is
    Silence; — that you may be receptive to
    Interior guidance, and that loving union reign.

2, Consecration *of the* Shrines.

(Attendant *Priests* lead the *Mystics* back into the first cave; the doors close. There the *Mystics* find papier-mache blocks with which they build their sanctuaries. Once *Camillus* begins to speak in answer to a beautiful *Maiden* who admires his work; and *Mysta* answers a *Priest* who benignantly suggests some improvement. Hereupon a terrible sudden wind-storm levels all that they have done. Then the *Mystics* begin again and silently complete their buildings. Then the doors open, and the *Mages* come out and inspect the buildings.)

NINTH, the SCARABÆUS

Magus, Congratulation on your sanctuaries
    Wherein your Guardian Powers may abide,
From where to see God's sun through your own glass,
    And where you find repose such as you need.
Maga, So let us dedicate each one in turn,
    And listen to what message you may hear.

A, CAMILLUS.

(At *Camillus's* sanctuary's wicket is placed a candle, and he enters. The door is shut, a flame descends and lights the candle. All other lights go out, and there is heard an Æolian harmony.)

Magus, We dedicate this sanctuary to light

Maga, And beauty, grace and heavenly renown.

Magus, May wisdom constantly within here dwell,

Maga, And may this prove the home of discipline.

Magus, May all twelve Silences this temple haunt,
    But Fancy's Silence specially be heard.

Maga, May all twelve Motives here be sanctified,
    And may the Quest of Beauty not disturb.

Magus, May all twelve Sins be kept without the door,
    But specially the Failing of Caprice.

Maga, May no Dislike, if knocking, entrance find,
    And Dulness meet the largest charity.

Magus, May all twelve Practices be exercised,
    But specially the one of Coming Death.

Maga, May all twelve Virtues find expression here,
    But most the Virtue of Harmoniousness.

Magus, May all twelve Principles be here lived out,
    But specially the Principle of Truth.

Maga, May life shed forth its full significance,
    But here reveal itself as absolute!

Magus, [knocks,] Come out, my Son, tell us what was revealed,
Maga, That we may also profit by your gain.
Camillus, [coming out], What in the Ninth of Heavens I beheld
   Surpasses my ability to tell;
   Each heart, besides, has its own mysteries.
   But that which drew hot tears in agonies
   Was that these spiritual experiences
   Dogmas become, to persecutions lead;
   Father, is there no way to save the Church?
Magus, My Son, it is destiny, but not yet fate.
Camillus, What if I did my best to find the way?
Maga, Like every other savior, you would die.
Camillus, Then must I rouse men lulled to living wrong,
   Relying on salvation magical.
Magus, My Child, I see the shade of Death on you.
Maga, Be moderate; if you would live to serve!
[to *Priests*] Has Persius MICHAEL deserved a crown?
Priests,   He has!
Magus, Then, MICHAEL, kneel, accept our prayers;
   We crown you a *Courier of the Sun,*
   A Missionary Pilgrim of the Light.
Priests, Amen!
   (To his breast is pinned a golden Scarabæus.)

B, MYSTA.

Maga, We dedicate this sanctuary to Love,
Magus, And holy Wisdom in its exercise.
Maga, May holy purposes within here dwell,
Magus, And holier grow by constant discipline.

NINTH, the SCARABÆUS

Maga, May all twelve Silences this Temple haunt,
  But most the one of Meanness cowardly.

Magus, May all twelve Motives here be sanctified,
  And kindliness not overwhelm the right!

Maga, May all twelve Sins be kept outside the door
  Justification-of-Oneself the most!

Magus, May no dislike, though knocking, entrance find,
  Fear of Foolhardiness the most!

Maga, May all twelve Practices be exercised the most
  But specially the one of Rectitude!

Magus, May all twelve Virtues find expression here,
  But most Cooperation's magic wand!

Maga, May all twelve Principles be here lived out,
  But specially Endurance here be learned!

Magus, May Life shed forth its full significance,
  And here become symbolical of Love!

Maga, [knocks,] Daughter, come out, relate what
  was revealed,

Magus, That also we may profit by your gain.

Mysta, [comes out,] What in the Ninth of Heavens
  I beheld
    Surpasses lawfulness of utterance;
    Besides, each heart has its own mysteries.
    But that which drew hot tears in agony
    Were sacred Love's vile degradations,
    Its masquerades, abuses and disgrace,
    Forgetting it is immortality.

Magus, My Child, your grief is an immortal one.

Mysta, Yet could a woman savior not assist
  By teaching woman's rights and dignity?

Maga, Ages will pass before that victory;
  Yet every teacher hastens on that Day.

NINTH, the SCARABAEUS

Mysta, None but a God could undertake that work!
Maga, You are that god, and shall by Gods be helped!
Mysta, Then that shall be the mission of my life.
Maga, And martyrdom, for thou wouldst not escape.
Mysta, The sooner would I enter martyrs' heaven.
Magus, Has Persius-MYSTA now deserved a crown?
Priests,   She has!
Magus, Then, MYSTA, kneel, accept our prayers,
    We crown you a *Courier of the Moon,*
    A Missionary Pilgrim of the Stars!
Priests,   Amen!

    (To her breast is pinned a golden Scarabæus.)

Chorus, Mayest thou be beneficent like the Lord of Holiness,

    Mayest thou be glorious, like the Good Shepherd,
    Mayest thou be able to reach the far shore of the Cloud-Sea on the Mountain of Serene Abode,
    Mayest thou become such that the heavenly Halo will cling to thee,
    Mayest thou be beloved by the Gods, and revered by men,
    Mayest thou find entrance to the bright, all-happy, blissful abode of the Saints!

    May it happen to thee according to my blessing,
    That sickness never threaten thy good health,
    That thou grow long-lived like some venerable sage!
    Let us adopt and propagate God's good thoughts, good words and good deeds,
    That have been done, and will be done, here and elsewhere,
    That we may be found among the number of the good,
    Mayest thou follow the law of Truth,
    Mayest thou achieve Paradise alive!

3, *The* Instruction.

Magus, In each Degree you learned the lesson of
    One of the parts of your own organism;
    This time you learn the secrets of your Chest,
    By studying the habits of the Crab,
    Who grows into a sacred Scarabee
    By basking in the sanctifying sun.

Maga, Lovers of home are crabs; while scarabees
    Transform this home into a sanctuary
    Which here you learned to build and consecrate.

Magus, But how to use it you must also learn:
    The minimum is what you would have done
    Had you invited home some honored guest.
    You would protect him from intrusions,
    Give him an invitation definite,
    Meetings appoint at times convenient.
    At least not less than this must you have done
    Would you attract some heavenly Presences.

Maga, This is the secret why so many find
    Their sanctuaries empty, nude and bare.
    They think the heavenly Powers will remain
    Accessible, just like some furniture,
    While they themselves go out, or work at will,
    Reentering when fancy may dictate.

Magus, And of the many times when God will come
    The best and the most natural is dawn,
    When even birds their orisons perform,
    And visions most veridical abound.
    Next is the dusk, or at the hour of noon;
    Most powerful of all, the midnight hour.

        (A gong strikes twelve.)

4, Revelation *and* its Results.

Maga, There is a further secret due to you
    Which cannot be revealed by word of mouth,
    But may be given you in sanctuary:
    Enter, and try to learn that mystic word!

(Silence, the *Mystics* cry, Enoch! Elijah! Iqibala! Quetzalcoatl! Yudisthira!)

Mysta, I see the heavenly chariot of fire
    Rise from the desert near the Jordan's bank;
    And I behold the Messengers of Heaven
    Driving the horses shod with lightning hue!

Camillus, Tell more!

Mysta, Of Saviors yet a higher rank I see,
    Higher than those who with the dragons fought:
    Those who were translated while alive.
    This is the secret of the Ninth Degree:
    Saviors unseen surround us night and day;
    But we are blind until in sanctuary
    We are protected from the outside world.
    Wherefore, when entering in a room that you
    Desire to consecrate, close all the doors,
    And praying at each opening, draw the line
    Of magic fire that Opponents frights;
    There are you safe so long as quite awake,
    Or not forgetful of the Presences.

Mysta, I see that we must join their ranks,
    For they, outside, are beckoning to us;
    Come, let us follow, ere they pass away!

(Both *Mystics* issue from their sanctuaries, and stand in the right opening of the Cave, stretching forth their hands, pleading)

Mystics, O Presences, depart not yet from us!

NINTH, *the* SCARABAEUS

    Must we be left as soon as we have seen
    Some fluttering fringe of your celestial robe?
    Forsake us not unto ourselves, to grieve!
    Will you return? Alas, the skies stay dark!

Maga, Not they will ever come again to you;
    You are the ones who must go after them, —
    Upon the peak you must their coming wait.

Camillus, I thought our shrines were built to be our homes,
    But now, as soon as we acquire them,
    You speak of leaving them behind!

Magus, Spiritual homes are shrines, not physical;
    Not residence, nor fortress permanent;
    Shrines are not built to hinder your advance,
    They are stations for refreshment on the road,
    They are *homes* only for such as *stay* behind.

Mysta, But how can I forsake my sanctuary?
    At least from time to time I would return!

Maga, That is just why, that you may stay up there,
  Lest some dark Tempter lure you back down here.
    You must block up this Cave, preventing fall.
    Though sacred are the altars of your vows,
    You now are vowed unto a higher quest;
    Your only safety lies in sudden flight.

Mysta, The entrance shall be blocked; but tell us how!

Maga, That is a problem which yourselves must solve!
  (The *Mystics* look around for beams or stones; in vain.)

Camillus, Nothing is to be found; we come to you
    To help us to obey your own command.

Magus, Ask not of me, but of your god within.

Mysta, Are not these Presences more sacred than
    Our former sanctuaries within the Cave?

NINTH, *the* SCARABÆUS

What if we used them to obstruct the door?

Maga, Not even sanctuaries are too divine
　　To act as barrier of the soul's return
　　Unto her past. So with the dignity
　　Of those who have beheld a higher sight,
　　Closing your eyes lest grief again should blind,
　　Fall on your sanctuaries and tear them down.
　　True, you will lose them, but for memory;
　　Just how you built them you will soon forget;
　　They would be meaner, should you try again;
　　The outline of the Pattern may be lost;
　　Your efforts will possess less grace and charm;
　　But you will stand on glorious mountain-peak,
　　Not in a cave reminding of your past; —
　　Fall on them quickly, lest your heart grow faint!

(Weeping, the *Mystics* rush to tear down the kiosks. To comfort them, the *Mages* sing a song of hope and faith, in which the *Mystics* join, as soon as their task is completed. The entrance is blocked, all but for the last piece which *Mysta* brings to *Maga*.)

Mysta, Mother, I do not dare to set this piece, —
　　It is the last reminder of my shrine.
　　I trust it only to your own dear hand, —
　　Pray for a blessing on our vandal deed!

Maga, Although yourself unconscious of the source,
　　It was an Angel who suggested this;
　　For as your Initiatress, I alone
　　Possess the right to seal your victory.
　　Ages shall bless you for your sacrifice;
　　Nations, someday, your names shall venerate,
For you have conquered; and in Heaven's name,
　　For ever, on your past, I set this crown!

――― 🪲 ―――

Questions to be Answered in Writing ✒ 9

Not to be answered all at once, but each on the indicated day of the month, overlapping from 22nd to 22nd.

The ideal time to study this Degree alone is in June to July. If the whole series is to be taken, it is best to begin on Dec 22.

But the first 22nd after you hear of these Degrees is the time Providence has set for *your* beginning; *anything* ranks delay.

Day 22, Read and copy the Degree, and memorize your favorite selections therefrom, and record them.

Day 23, What is the advantage in a sanctuary, — for man, and for the divine influence?

Day 24, Are any sanctuaries mentioned in the Bible? Recount the texts speaking of man as a temple.

Day 25, What biblical characters, on a mountain, saw the pattern of a shrine? Gather pictures.

Day 26, Why is silence needful for the building of a sanctuary?

Day 27, How can one consecrate a sanctuary?

Day 28, How does one draw a magic circle? Why is one sometimes necessary?

Day 29, What is the minimum standard of care suitable to a sanctuary? What is the maximum for ornaments? Where does the rule come from?

Day 30, What are the best times of day to meet the Presence in the sanctuary? At what times might the Unseen Helpers have the least conflicting engagements?

Day 1, Assign several reasons why so many find their sanctuaries empty?

Day 2, Tell the chief secret of the Ninth Degree.

Day 3, What is the highest rank of saviors? What is their peculiarity, and what does this sometimes entail on those who would follow them?

Day 4, The Druidesses of the mouth of the Loire used to destroy their sanctuaries annually; assign several good aspects of this.

Practical Experiments to be Reported 🙰 9

Day 5, Choose some spot where you can remain undisturbed, of which you have the exclusive use.

Day 6, Pray for divine approval or disapproval.

Day 7, Fit it up comfortably, with easy chair, and table for writing, and drawer to store papers, especially your *Experience Book,* crystal, & mirror. If possible provide a white gown or vestment.

Day 8, You may provide a picture, candle, incense-dish; but adopt the Japanese rule of a single one of each.

Day 9, Consecrate it by prayer,

Day 10, Exorcise all evil influences, magically sealing every opening.

Day 11, Arrange your affairs, and list what times for meetings are possible to you; midnight is best.

Day 12, Continue in prayer until you are assured which time is selected by the Highest Presence Available; only your Guardian Angel can meet you *at any time.* You are not the *only one!*

Day 13, Be sure to be on time; put on your vestment, do a little will-task, consult your crystal.

Day 14, Repeat, listen, look and feel for a definite pre-determined interval, to avoid passivity (spiritualistic mediumship entrancement) and dozing.

Day 15, Learn the attitude of treating the Presence with just as much consideration as you would give to an honored, desired, beloved guest.

Day 16, Learn the attitude of going through your routine regardless of success or failure, for the Presence always comes unexpectedly.

Day 17, If you expect regular results you must keep your appointment regularly, if for nothing else so that your subconsciousness can form a habit.

Day 18, If the keeping of an engagement would entail some expense, remember that God is rich, and is both **able** and willing to repay.

TENTH DEGREE

The Eagle

Soul-Marriage to Wisdom

The Mithraic Mysteries, Modernized.

Tenth Degree, the Eagle.

Major Points

1 **Symbol**, the Eagle.
2 **Purpose**, Magic Evocation.
3 **Scene**, The High Mountain-side.
4 **Peculiarity**, Solitude was only kindness.
5 **Temptation**, Discouragement.
6 **Oath**, Marriage to Wisdom.
7 **Divisions**,   1, The Need for Evocation.
    2, Evocation of, and Marriage to Wisdom.

Minor Points

1 **Element**, Fire.
2 **Sign**, Gemini, or Shoulders.
3 **Sign-parts**, Ophichuus, Orion, Sirius.
4 **Planet**, Neptune.
5 **Color**, Violet.
6 **Greek Philosophy**, Stoicism.
7 **Hindu Philosophy**, Yoga.
8 **Ethnic Religion**, Chinese, Confucianism.

The Tenth Degree

The Eagle, — Evocation.

1, Introduction.

(The *Mystics* are moodily sitting on two rocks, on the summit of the mountain. With some hesitation, from the right come the *Mages*.)

Magus, MYSTICS, all hail! We would be glad to know
   Of your successes during the last month.
Maga, Upon your countenances I dare read
That some of you have seen the heavenly Visitants.
Camillus, Alas, in vain our watches! We regret
   That we forsook our sanctuaries below;
   And were they not blocked up, we would return.
Mysta, Were we deceived by some disordered gust?
   Out in the world such watching could not be,
   Even if They should come.
Camillus,   Could we have seen
   Their forms by sight more keen, through magnifying glass?
Magus, I note that you have failed; but none of you
   Advanced the real cause why you have failed.
Maga, Were you not told to build a sanctuary
   Wherein, protected from disturbances,
   Your senses might the subtlest change perceive?
Camillus, Yes, but we lack materials for such house!

Magus, Draw nearer, and observe how I create
 Conditions right to make GOD visible!

Mysta, So oft already we have tried in vain!

Maga, Just once too little is your plaint, 'So oft!'
 For now to you I here shall demonstrate
 That GOD is present here, so that the fault
 Lay with your ignorance how to detect.
   (*Magus* raises his arms,)

Magus, Father, who once didst hear Elishah's prayer
 That his young man might see thy Guardian Host,
 Of these two MYSTICS open Thou the eyes,
 That they gain faith in thy Protecting Love!
 (From behind, *Maga* holds her hands over *Mysta's* eyes)

Maga, Utter your vision!

Mysta,   I behold this hill
 Crowded with serried ranks of shining forms!
 Upon us cloven tongues of fire descend!
 The stars are peering straight into my soul!
   (*Magus,* holding his hands over *Camillus's* eyes,)

Magus,   Speak!

Camillus, I see the Heavens' central Sanctuary:
 A perfect sphere upon a pediment;
 And, at the top, upsoaring angel-flights!
 Around, the gleaming sentinels
 Repelled whoever came without a vow.
 In white procession, I behold a nebula
 Of all the aspirations of my life!

Mysta, (bursts out with enthusiasm,) Your Guardian
 Angels, bringing flowers, approach!
 Oh now I understand our First Degree!
 There we refused all earthly crowns to wear,
 Not to conflict with amaranthine wreaths!
Who would suspect our Guides meant what they said,

That *crown of Truth* meant genuine astral flowers?
   But all has disappeared! MAGES, I pray,
   Once more impose your hands upon my brow!
Maga, It cannot be! All help from outer source
   Is accidental and temporary!
   What we have done was to convince you both
   That solitude alone is of small help.
   Enlightenment is permanent only when
   Quite independent of external aid;
   When man has learned to make conditions right
   And knows how to detect the spirit-world,
   It ne'er will waver from his stumbling side.
Mysta, Teach us to do so without outside help
   Of temple, or of initiating guide!
Magus, Such evocation now will we attempt:
   Yourselves the magic circle shall erect.

2, *The* Evocation.

(The *Mages,* veiling themselves, sit down on some stones in the centre, and give directions which the *Mystics* follow. They make alternate twelfths of a magic circle, *Camillus* repeating the words of *Magus,* and *Mysta* those of *Maga.* The *Mystics* veil themselves. The *Mages* raise their arms. As the *Mystics* proceed around the circle, they leave behind a phosphorescent trail which glows only so long as the prayers continue, after which it dies down. The *Mages* give the *Mystics* edible biscuit tablets.)

Magus, Upon these tablets quickly write in full
   What definite questions in your hearts revolve:
   Or how can you expect the Answerers
   To satisfy cravings indefinite?
   Now set the tablets down in full plain sight!
Maga, Another warning note ere we begin.

TENTH, *the EAGLE*

The least contention or distraction will
At once destroy the power of miracle.
So we we begin with hymns, while holding hands,
Creating thus full unanimity.   [All sing]

THE EVOCATION

Depart not yet, stay near a little longer,
  O holy Visitors from heavenly shore;
  Utter again, with virtue yet far stronger,
  Your benedictions, ere our prayers be o'er.

We would detain you in our midst forever,
  If this could be, with souls not yet beyond;
  Each has his quest, which following will sever
  This magic circle's sacramental bond.

Yet once more raise your arms in benediction,
  Yet once more speak the secret word of might;
  Yet once more heal our weary heart's affliction,
  And for one moment touch our sense-bound sight.

Then once more stand aside while He who sent you
  From midst your band reveal His blessed Face;
So shall we thank both you and Him who sent you
  To be the channels of his heavenly hosts.

Magus, Now let us share your tablets, that we all
  May actively resist low influence.
  Your questions have been seen, and will
  Answers attract from spiritual Guides.

Maga, Attention! Now each in his turn repeat

Magus, In Unity the Daemons chant the praises of God, they lose their malice and fury,—*Glory for ever and ever, Amen!*

Maga, By the Duad, the Zodiacal Fishes chant the praises of God as the thunder and lightning fuse in

TENTH, *the* EAGLE

harmonious, blessing rain, — *Glory for ever and ever, Amen!*

Magus, The Fiery Serpents of the Hermetic Caduceus interlace three times; Cerberus opens his triple jaw, and three-pronged is Neptune's Trident which drives the Dolphins that chant the praises of God, — *Glory for ever and ever, Amen!*

Maga, At the Fourth Hour of Night the soul revisits the tombs; the magical lamps are lighted at the four corners of the circle, in the four seasons of illusions and enchantments, *Glory for ever and ever, Amen!*

Magus, The voice of the great Five Oceans celebrates the God of the Heavenly Spheres, *Glory for ever, and ever, Amen!*

Maga, The Spirit believes itself immortal; it beholds the Six Infernal Monsters, and stamps upon them; for it does not fear, chanting the praise of God, —*Glory for ever and ever, Amen!*

Magus, The Seven Undivulged Irrational Numbers chant the praises of God, who in the seven primary colors coruscates differently on each of the seven days of the week, — *Glory for ever and ever, Amen!*

Maga, By the Ogdoad of Abysmal Fulness, by the Aeons that limit and crucify, by the eight tears of Sophia, the Redeemer of the Ages chants the praises of God, — *Glory for ever and ever, Amen!*

Magus, A Fire which imparts life to all animated beings is directed and centred by the wills of Three Triads of Pure United Men. The Initiate stretches forth his hands, and the Nine Pains he assuages, and the Nine Stars of Cassiopea chant the praises of God, — *Glory for ever and ever, Amen!*

Maga, The ten cyclic rejuvenations of the microcosm and macrocosm ebb and flow over the ten mountains of Atlantis, and ten are the Patriarchs who hand down the Past to the Future, chanting the praises of God, — *Glory for ever and ever, Amen!*

Magus, The eleven wings of the Genii, the eleven plumes of the Cherubim, and the eleven gills of the Leviathan move with a mysterious sweep, emitting a sonorous murmur, chanting the aeolian praises of God, — *Glory for ever and ever, Amen!*

Maga, The Twelve Constellations commune in an ecliptic cadence; the Soul of the Sun responds to the fragrance of the flowers of each of the Twelve Months of the year; the silver chains of the twelve Lunar Harmonies summate the correspondences between all natural things, in one vast acclaim, chanting the praises of God, — *Glory for ever and ever, Amen!*

Magus, What question, CAMILLUS?

Camillus, Wisdom I demand!

(He is startled; he looks upward, his gaze is fixed as if he beheld something unseen. *Magus* produces a ring, with a stone suitable to his birth-month, and slips on *Camillus's* left-hand ring-finger. He sinks on his left knee, with left hand extended in air. Prompted by *Magus* he repeats)

Camillus, 'I take thee, heavenly WISDOM, for my wife,
Henceforth forever, till my day of death!'
(Ineffable bliss transfigures his being.)
'To thee I vow a faithfulness supreme
In sickness, health, in sorrow and in joy;
For thee let me provide within my home,
Only remain within my reverent reach!'

TENTH, *the* EAGLE

Wisdom [from above,] This is my only wedding-gift
                              to thee,
   That thou shalt know My presence when the tears
      Spring out all unforeseen, and dim the sight.
      Holier, CAMILLUS, is the serious face
         Than that of smiles and laughter, which becomes
      Wild grief; and if in sorrow thou desire
         To see My face, My counsel to receive,
      Then shall I come to comfort thee within.
Camillus, [wildly], Depart not from me, Splendor
                              aureate!
Wisdom, CAMILLUS, my name is Wisdom from the
                              Heavens!
   I come whenever it is wise for thee;
   I also leave, whenever it is best.
   If men wish to possess Me evermore
   Then must they form a constant need of Me,
   Of earnest Wisdom to some needy soul.
   Wherefore live thou a life of charity
      And ministration unto those in need;
      And as thou servest humble, simple souls
   I will be found of thee beside thy steps,
And hold thee up, when stumbling thou mightst fall.
Camillus, My God, my God, why hast thou forsaken
                              me?
         (Weeps, covers his head with his veil.)

Maga, What question, MYSTA?

Mysta,   Wisdom also come!

(She gazes upward with a rapt expression as if seeing a beatific vision. *Maga* produces a ring suitable to *Mysta's* August birth-month, and slips it on to her left ring-finger. *Mysta* kneels on her left knee, and with left hand extended in air, prompted by *Maga,* she cries,)

Mysta, I take thee, Heavenly Wisdom, for my mate
    Henceforth and ever till my day of death;
    I vow to thee a faithfulness supreme
    In sickness, health, in sorrow and in joy.
    For thee let me provide within my home;
    Only remain within my reverent reach!

Wisdom, This is my only marriage-gift to thee,
    The magic secret how to summon Me;
    Not by the heart's too passionate desire,
    But by the leash of constant discipline
    Will I be bound to thee, my human bride!
    So, when desiring Me, then practise thou
    An hour of silence, and an hour of work;
    And as thy will-task thou accomplishest
    Before thou knowest I will stand near thee.
    This is the secret that controls My steps, —
    Lo, even God has bound Himself to men; —
    Forget it not, when overwhelmed with grief!

Mysta, I will not let thee from me; I demand......

(Suddenly all goes out. Desirous of beholding the Divinity, *Camillus* had removed his veil, and in doing so had inadvertently put his foot outside the magic circle. *Mysta* faints; the *Mages* revive her. *Camillus* readjusts his veil, restores the magic circle and repeats the *Nuktemeron.*)

Mysta, Leave thou me not, I am not strong enough!

Wisdom, Daughter and Wife, thy soul is strong enough
    For what is right and wise, because divine;
    Lo, I have given thee power over God, —
    Use it discreetly, and with reverence!
    Six times obey the thought of some you scorn,
    Six times relieve some needy suffering,......
  Crusading quests like these bring the Holy Grail!
    Thou who hast thought to attract the world,
    Only for love's sweet sake shalt thou attain!

TENTH, *the* EAGLE

> So God becomes thy bride; and like a bride,
> Weak in her heart, I long to come to thee.
> Ah, disappoint Me not! But, every night,
> Bring Me thy heart, that I may comfort it:
> And flying thus direct unto the Sun,
> Then shall you *Father-Eagles* have become!

Mages, Our arms are weary; spite of us they fall!
    No longer can we raise this prayer for you!

(Thunder and lightning, darkness. There is still heard diminishing echoes of voices singing, *Glory for ever and ever, Amen!*)

Chorus, We celebrate the cosmic nuptial mysteries
    Whereby to Mithra souls assimilation find,
    By education mating with next higher angel-rank
    The which in turn with starward impulse aquiline
    From chaos-wandering comet gravitates into
A satellitic planetary mood which, worshipfully lured,
    Shall someday hurtle into its cynosure,
    From twin-stage fusing into a married phoenix-pyre
    Wherefrom in newer era shall arise a newer world,
As the Archangels Seven fused in God Supreme.

    Be not, O Human Soul, like Virgins insensate
Who, waiting for the Bridegroom at the midnight hour,
    Too late discovered that their oil was low;
    And seeking more, the Bridegroom's coming missed!
    Be not, O Human Soul, like an invited guest
    Who to the marriage-feast refused to come,
Distracted by the oxen and the fields he would acquire;
    Fruitless shall he remain, and die alone!

    Like eaglet staring at the Central Sun,
    Dart towards the zenith, apotheosis seek,
    Growing divine by Marriage of the Mind!

—— II ——

Questions to be Answered in Writing 🖉 10

Not to be answered all at once, but each on the indicated day of the month, overlapping from 22nd to 22nd.

The ideal time to study this Degree alone is in May to June. If the whole series is to be taken, it is best to begin on Jan. 22.

But the first 22nd after you hear of these Degrees is the time Providence has set for *your* beginning; *anything* ranks delay.

Day 22, Read and copy the Degree, and memorize your favorite selections therefrom, and record them.

Day 23, Mention scriptural examples of loneliness rooted in blindness.

Day 24, Mention daily life instances of methods, right and wrong, of temporarily heightening the the spiritual faculties, such as the Mages used.

Day 25, Relate the vision of heaven of Camillus, of any other person you may have known, or of yourself, if you have been so privileged.

Day 26, Explain the only now understandable deeper meaning of the First Degree.

Day 27, Gather the biblical and other parables describing salvation as a divine marriage of the soul.

Day 28, How did the neophytes manage to get answers to their questions?

Day 29, Memorize and reproduce Apollonius's *Nuktemeron*, and study its significance.

Day 30, What is the secret how to keep Wisdom near you constantly?

Day 1, How can one summon divine Wisdom?

Day 2, What accident can break up the divine vision and why?

Day 3, By what methods does the soul-marriage take place?

Day 4, Why should every man have a nightly hour of prayer?

Practical Experiments to be Reported 🖉 10

Day 5, Make lists of divine and holy things occurring in groups of 1, 2, 3, 4, 5, and 6.

Day 6, Continue the work with groups of 7 to 12.

Day 7, Read *How to Imprison Angels* (in *Manual*.)

Day 8, On the same subject, *How to attract Angels, and to make them Visible*, write an essay or poem.

Day 9, Practise your own methods till you achieve successful results.

Day 10, Make yourself a Hebrew High-priest's *ephod* and use it as they did.

Day 11, Explain how Charity prepares the soul for wisdom. Make an experiment, and record results.

Day 12, Will-tasks clear the mind for reception of wisdom. Make an experiment, rnd record results.

Day 13, Read, marginally marking favorite passages with pencil, *Ecclesiastes*, the apocryphal *Wisdom*, Paul's *Corinthians* and *Ephesians*, and *James*.

Day 14, Read Guthrie's *Marriage of Love and Wisdom*, and the biblical *Song of Solomon*. Then write your own love-song to Wisdom.

Day 15, Make suitable festal preparations in your sanctuary for your soul-marriage; provide a ring with your birth-stone.

Day 16, Marry your soul to Wisdom, and note the interior response.

Day 17, Decide on some one supreme question in your life, to which you desire a divine answer. Write it out fully, in definite, exact language. Pray for a divine answer, spread the paper on your sanctuary table, and lock the door.

Day 18, Prayerfully listen till you get an answer.

ELEVENTH DEGREE

The Father

Choice of Successors

The Mithraic Mysteries, Modernized.

Eleventh Degree, the Father.

Major Points

1 **Symbol**, the Father.
2 **Purpose**, Missionary Career.
3 **Scene**, The High Mountain-top.
4 **Peculiarity**, Inability to proceed until successors are chosen.
5 **Temptation**, To use the Power of Evocation selfishly.
6 **Oath**, To care for the Future of Humanity.
7 **Divisions**, 1, Introduction. 2, The Revelation. 3, The Appointment. 4, The Election.

Minor Points

1 **Element**, Fire.
2 **Sign**, Taurus, or Neck (cerebellum and glands).
3 **Sign-parts**, Bootes, Corona, Pleiades.
4 **Planet**, Comets.
5 **Color**, Blue.
6 **Greek Philosophy**, Hermetism.
7 **Hindu Philosophy**, Purva Mimansa.
8 **Ethnic Religion**, Mohammedan Resignation.

The Eleventh Degree

The Father — Missionary Career.

1, The Introduction.

(It is night, on the mountain-peak. In the distance below are seen the lights of the Temple of Æsculapius at Pergamum. The lights flicker out. All are assembled on the mountain-peak, and the *Mages* prepare to leave.)

Camillus, Father and Brother, leave us not alone:
    We love you, and we need your criticism,
    For we are trying to improve ourselves.
    (Affectionately *Mysta* approaches *Maga,* and whispers,)
Mysta, Because we would be initiated now
    Into the Eleventh Heaven of the Gods.
Magus, Last month you reached equality with us
    Becoming *Father-Eagles* of the Sun;
    How should we initiate our equal Gods?
    Besides, how know you there is aught beyond?
    Fortunate they who have attained all things!
Camillus, Unfortunate are they who who *think* they have!
    I may not know, but I have great desire;
    I hear strange voices, and I visions see.
Mages, According to your sight be it to you:
    Therefore for you an initiation waits!
Maga, But you, my Daughter, fortunate are you
Who reached contentment, and therewith your end!

ELEVENTH; *the FATHER*

Mysta, But I would formulate a practical
   Arrangement of its truths for all the world!
Maga, Then, Daughter, you have trials yet to bear.
Mysta, I prophesy there is another heaven:
   I feel the double dart that stings my soul!
Maga, My child, I pity you; yet wish you joy!
   How recklessly divine are hnman souls
   That grasp the very heaven of heavens before
   They have grown worthy of the nearest step!
   But as your faith, such is your destiny!
   Sans any fear stretch out your blind man's cane
   No doubt some passing angels will direct.
Camillus, Then you will initiate without delay?
Magus, [sternly,] Silence! Recall this utterance, or
      we leave!
Mysta, [grieved,] As you direct; we know that you
      are wtse,
   But set us on the road thereto, at least!
Maga, Your Father-brother has already said
   We could no longer initiate your souls
   Because our equals you have now become.
   And more; it is a month since you have been
   Married to Wisdom; should we interfere?
   From her seek light; lest, growing jealous, she
   Forsake your souls, and nevermore return.
   From her seek initiation, if you think
   There be a Heaven you have not attained.
Magus, Dear Children, though we gladly would have
      stayed
   Close by your side while further you progressed,
   To punish you, (that is, because you showed
   You needed stronger measures to insure
   A safer passage to the further heaven,)
   We will abandon you to your own selves.

Maga, That is, unto your Heavenly Bride! Farewell!
　　But ere we go, raise up your hands and swear
　　Never to seek for wisdom but within,
　　And to be faithful to your Heavenly Bride!

Mystics, We swear full faithfulness unto our Bride!

Mages, Now you are safe, we leave you here, farewell!

2, *The* Revelation.

Camillus, There is no hope for us but in ourselves,
　　So each must plan the heaven that he seeks.

Mysta, I will obey, and Heavenly Wisdom call,
　　Drawing her down to us by bands of love.
　　'Married to Thee, we suck at thy high sphere,
　　And dare Thee fail to manifest in us.
　　Where art Thou now? Where it is best for us;
　　Our need of Thee is of thy presence proof.'

Camillus, Let us again the magic circle draw!

(With a cane he draws a line over the earth, leaving a mark, chanting the *Nuktemeron,* as in the former Degree. *Mysta* takes the second verse, and so alternately to the end. Then both cry)

Mystics, WISDOM in thought, thy presence we adjure;
　　Wisdom in deed, we represent thy form;
　　Wisdom in word, we call Thee by thy name!

(A flame falls down upon the altar, and there is heard a *Voice*)

Voice, Wisdom is ever present unto prayer;
　　There is no initiation but within;
　　No soul can enter in the Inner Gate
　　Till she have found another pilgrim soul
　　To take her place upon the Stair of Heaven;
　　Wherefore, until you have successors brought,
　　You cannot be promoted further on!
　　　　(The flame dies down.)

Camillus, To find successors at this time and place
  We certainly will need interior powers!
Mysta, Our consciousness will have to roam the world
  Discovering whatever souls are ripe;
  It must be love that shall supply the wings!
Camillus, But magic presence must the pilot be;
  Within the crystal jewel of our rings
  Perhaps we'll see the souls that we adjure.
Mysta, But first we must intoxicate each one
  With the desire to help, redeem and save.
Camillus, The magic of the pen I'll wield, as scribe.
Mysta, While I make choice of those who need us most,
  Cov'ring my eyes that I may better see
  Whom WISDOM chooses and commends to us.
Camillus, So let it be; let us begin at once.

2, The Evocation.

(*Camillus* blindfolds *Mysta* who sits down in the centre.)

Mysta, Heavenly WISDOM, source of light and trust,
  Help us to find successors in these rites!
Camillus, Beneath us, at the Mountain's foot,
  I see the Æsculapian Temple's lights.
  Within, I note the sleeping forms of those
  Who come to pass the night in vision's trance,
  Gathered about the tripod of their God.
  Their choice has chosen them as candidates;
  Let us therefore adjure them to approach!
Mysta, So do; but as to me, my choice is made;
  MYSTUS's countenance, imploring help,
  Pursues me till I help him to succeed.

Camillus, And so will I: at once unto the work!
    Let us observe the inside of our rings,
    Imagining the letters of his name,
    And then pronounce them!

(The *Mystics* pick up twigs or wands, and on the earth trace the letters, as *Mysta* pronounces them.)

    MYSTUS, we summon you to show your form;
    Wise is obedience to the call of love!
    Suddenly leave thy body's resting-place.
    Though great the effort, dare the steep ascent
    Upward o'er rocks and through the dark ravines.
    Spirit of MYSTUS, we compel thee here!

(Wan and pale, wringing his hands in grief, *Mystus's* spirit appears outside the circle of fire, wandering around, seeking ingress. To him *Mysta* stretches out her hands, but he does not recognize her, and she grieves.)

Camillus, MYSTA, beware lest you erase the marks,
    Or he will flee before our work is done;
    Then how shall we the Temple-sleepers reach,
    Ignoring as we do their several names?

Mysta, The kerchief round my eyes still firmer bind
    Still more to clear my vision; on my brow
    Your hand shall guide my spirit's quest,
    Observing some distinctive mark of each;
    We shall thereto appeal.
        [*Camillus* does so.]
            On mantle red
    The letter **R** a girl distinguishes.
        [*Camillus* writes the letter.]

Camillus, Sleeper whose name is **R**, approach us here!
[There approaches a pale young girl with a bluish light on her forehead.]

Mysta, There is a man whose garments bear no mark,
    His hair is white, a scar is on his cheek.

[*Camillus* writes 'Scar.']

Camillus, Spirit with scar on cheek, and white on hair,
 Come at our call, and climb the paths of heaven!
Mysta, Three Thracians more; a man, a boy; a girl;
 I see no names; the man wears three rich rings,
 The girl has jeweled pins; around his neck,
 The boy a bulla wears.

(*Mysta's* eyes are released; *Camillus* writes.)

Camillus, Thracian, thrice-ringed, come to our magic fire!
 Boy with the bulla, hitherward ascend!
 Girl with the jewelled pin, fearlessly climb!

3, The Appointment.

Camillus, Now we begin to choose. Dear MYSTUS, first.
 Look in your ring, O MYSTA, see what appears!
(She breaks into tears; *Camillus* tries to comfort her.)

Mysta, I see that he will fail again next year.
 If he must fail, then also I shall stay.
 He shall not be forsaken in his grief;
 See, I shall step outside this line of fire!
Voice, Beware, INITIATE! See, thy return
 Him would not save, though thee it would destroy!
Mysta, A selfish heaven were torture unto me;
 My heaven shall be to stay with those that mourn!
Voice, Specious the plea, but founded on mistake.
 To give away good conscience were a sin;
 To help thy brother, fit thyself therefor,—
 Thus both are healed, instead of both in pain;
 Safely to WISDOM him thou may'st entrust!

ELEVENTH, *the FATHER*

(At the beginning was seen a fiery two-edged sword, held by a hand; gradually the remainder of the supporting figure, revealing the heavenly virgin *Wisdom* who after a moment of dazzling radiance vanishes.)

Camillus, MYSTA revered, if MYSTUS dear must fail,
    Then must you choose some other in his place.

Mysta, Choose you another one for me; he shall
    Not say I chose some other soul for heaven!

Wisdom, Thyself must make another choice, or else
    Thyself cannot progress to whence it may
    Sometime bring down salvation for thy friend.

Mysta, Then, for his sake, I choose some other soul;
    A soul as like to his as possible!

(From the souls wandering inconsolably around the fire, she seizes on the soul marked *R,* the man vainly seeking to escape.)

Mysta, **R**-man, I choose thee for the rites,
    And though yon MYSTUS hate, him shall you help!

[*R's* eyes suddenly open and shine with joy; he kneels down and raises his arms in prayer.]

Camillus, Release him, Mysta, from our circle's chain;
    It is the letter **R** that holds him fast.

(As the letter is erased, his spirit leaps up waving his arms, springing into space, leaving a track of light. *Mystus* is seen rushing down the rocks, disappearing into the darkness, but guided by a *Shining Figure.*)

Camillus, I choose the white-haired man with scar
                                   on cheek.
    From tribulation great he seems to come;
    Look in your ring, and see if he succeeds!

Mysta, Within my ring I see a shining crown!

(*Camillus* manages to lay hold on him; his eyes open, his face shines, and he kneels in prayer.)

Camillus, Release him, Mysta, from our circle's chain;
It is the **scar** that holds him bound to us.

[He raises his hands, while the *Mystics* cry *Persius! Persius!* His forehead shines, he bursts out into tears.]

Scar-Spirit, I do not wish to leave your holy band,
  You gods who summoned me from out my flesh;
  Let me remain with you upon the Mount!

Camillus, SPIRIT, depart! Also your day shall come;
  But first you must endure what Fates demand.
  Farewell! Persius! Persius!

[Slowly the *Scar-Spirit* goes down to the Temple, often looking back and waving greetings. The *Mystics* show emotion and manifest surprise at seeing him joined by three *Shining Figures* who softly sing Mendelsson's *Lift Thine Eyes*. Then from afar, as the cocks crow, shouts the]

Scar-Spirit, I prophesy the dawn! And I invoke
  The Powers of Heaven upon our future work;
  I go to help, to heal, to die, to rise!

[The dawn breaks. The other spirits suddenly cry, *Help! Help! Save us also here!* The *Initiates* grieve at not being able to help them, and hold their hands before their eyes. As the dawn slowly rises the *Shining Ones* who are holding the weeping Thracian family try to comfort them and lead them away, disappearing into the light that sifts onto the stage. As the day breaks fully the magic fire seems to die down; and issuing from the Mountain are heard the following *Choruses* of]

Womens' Voices, O Lord, most beneficent Spirit,
  Maker of the material world, thou holy One,
  What is the single prayer in which resides
  The greatest blessing proceeding from the Good
        Principle?

  He who faithfully and devotedly recites a prayer
        for holiness,
  He praises Me, the Lord of Knowledge;
  Because prayer for holiness increases the soul's
        strength and victory.
  It is worth a dozen sacrifices, when prayed while
        falling asleep;
  It is worth a hundred sacrifices, when prayed while
        eating, thus making a sacrament;
  It is worth a thousand sacrifices, when prayed while
        celebrating the rites of love;

ELEVENTH, *the* FATHER

It is worth a million sacrifices, when prayed while departing this life;
That is how the **Prayer for Holiness** is the secret of all other prayers.

Mens' Voices, O Lord, accept the words of this our prayer,
These words that I utter so imploringly;
For strength and vigor, all victorious,
For power of health and healing,
For fulness, increase, and graceful growth;
Bring them together with the words of hymns
Upon the sacred Mountain of the Lord:
Therefore I shall not ever fear to pray;
And thus in joy of perfect holiness
So shall I fearless pass the Judgment Bridge;
Kept perfectly, as by Thy virtue kept,—
Praise the Lord who keeps and maintains the moon and the sun!

Mysta, CAMILLUS, our own salvation now almost assured,
Must not make us forgetful of the lost;
Until we leave these rites each morn and night
An intercession must we raise to Heaven
For those whom we were forced to leave behind.
Until we pass beyond, they hold a claim
Upon our further progress spiritual.
Oh grim necessity, that some must fail!
For their own sakes especially, we must
Win power to save, and help them save themselves;
And saving others, *Father-Hawks* become!

(In the sunlight are seen the receding forms of the *Shining Ones*, who are reconducting the rejected souls down the mountain. Longingly the *Initiates* cry after them, *Mystus! Thracian! Bulla-boy! Breast-pin Girl!* As the light grows full, they all vanish.)

Questions to be Answered in Writing 🕮 11

Not to be answered all at once, but each on the indicated day of the month, overlapping from 22nd to 22nd.

The ideal time to study this Degree alone is in April to May. If the whole series is to be taken, it is best to begin on Feb 22.

But the first 22nd after you hear of these Degrees is the time Providence has set for *your* beginning; *anything* ranks delay.

Day 22, Read and copy the Degree, and memorize your favorite selections therefrom, and record them.

Day 23, Memorize and reproduce the *Adjuration to Wisdom.*

Day 24, Explain the significance of crystal-gazing, wearing and use of jewels, and magic mirrors.

Day 25, Are they truly fortunate who have achieved all their desires? Explain results.

Day 26, What does Fate reserve for any who have made a plan? Why does Fate do so?

Day 27, Why may we fearlessly *stretch out our blind man's cane?*

Day 28, May those who are married to Wisdom ask counsel of men? How far? Is obedience right?

Day 29, If you are seeking heaven, what must **you** do to reach it?

Day 30, Before we can be promoted, what must **we** find?

Day 1, What soul-ability does this imply?

Day 2, Explain Wisdom's seal.

Day 3, How can you best strengthen interior sight?

Day 4, How can you best help your friends, — for companionship with them, or to humor their fancy, to cease spiritual achievement; or, even in spite of them, to achieve the power to help them?

Practical Experiments to be Reported 🔖 11

Day 5, Take in your pocket lumps of sugar for horses, peanuts for squirrels, or seeds for birds.

Day 6, Put out water for birds and dogs, and observe the spiritual results.

Day 7, Judiciously relieve what requests for physical assistance come to you.

Day 8, Continue this, giving chiefly spiritual responses.

Day 9, Study the lives of benefactors such as Martin of Tours, Elizabeth of Hungary, Francis de Sales, Florence Nightingale, Zoroaster, Gautama, Jesus.

Day 10, Prayerfully try to imitate some of them.

Day 11, Learn to recognize *signals of distress*, remembering that among the unspiritual they manifest chiefly as anger, pride, spite and malice.

Day 12, Scrutinize every person you meet for the *unspoken distress,* which is frequently the most pitiable, and the most deserving of relief.

Day 13, Read Leadbeater's *Invisible Helpers.*

Day 14, In meditation, learn to recognize such signals of distress, relieving them from the spiritual plane exclusively. Check up on results.

Day 15, In meditation take up some individual person you know of, and by receptive insight visualize his ideals, needs and probable fate.

Day 16, Discover what can be done from the spiritual side to turn that fate into a destiny.

Day 17, By prayer select some successor for every work you are doing. (For yourself this means release and promotion.)

Day 18, From the spiritual plane prepare and fit him for it.

TWELFTH DEGREE

The Supreme Father

Unveiling of Final Truth

The Mithraic Mysteries, Modernized.

Twelfth Degree, the Supreme Father.

Major Points

1 **Symbol**, the Supreme Father.
2 **Purpose**, Unveiling of the Final Truth.
3 **Scene**, The Mountain-peak.
4 **Peculiarity**, One finds the Truth by *becoming* it.
5 **Temptation**, The Temple-Devil's suggestion that *there is no Truth*.
6 **Oath**, None, because nobody would believe the Truth; but there is a blood-writ challenge.
7 **Divisions**,
    1, Vision,
    2, The Gate of Humility,
    3, Temptation,
    4, Residuary Specializing Self-initiation.
    5, The Council,
    6, The Theophany,
    7, The Revelation of Truth,
    8, Farewells.

Minor Points

1 **Element**, Fire.
2 **Sign**, Aries, or Brain.
3 **Sign-parts**, Cassiopœa, Cetus, Triangulum.
4 **Planet**, The Central Sun of suns.
5 **Color**, Azure.
6 **Greek Philosopher**, Pythagoras.
7 **Hindu Philosophy**, Vedanta.
8 **Ethnic Religion**, Hercules and his 12 Labors, *The Two Ways*.

The Twelfth Degree

The Supreme Father, — Final Truth

(Scene, the peak of the Mystery Mountain.)

1, Vision.

Magus, Children and brethren, soon to be divine,
   Your intercessions strong have found a way
   Into the mystic Caverns of the Soul;
   And Presences around us beckon me
   To make you their successors on the Path.

Maga, The hour is here, the Master-workmen here,
   You also here, — one only thing now lacks, —
   That thing of course will never be supplied
   Until you guess it, and supply that need.

Camillus, We need a chant whose solemn fervor shall
   Draw tears from stars, and thrill the universe.

Mysta, Mother and Father, this one thing we need:
   The sanctuary wherein we may be shown
   Visions oracular, telestic rites.

(Silently she goes behind *Camillus,* lays her hand upon his forehead, and he describes what he sees.)

Camillus, Upon this barren Mount I see a shrine,
   Within a court, surrounded by a wall
   Formed by the former sanctuaries we built.
   Then in the centre I behold a dome
   Resplendent with the shine of faces dim.
   The Ruling Spirit round the sanctuary

186 TWELFTH, *the SUPREME FATHER*

  Erects his tent where he may be approached;
  I hear the song of the Eternal Lodge
  Gushing through key-hole in the Mystic Door;
Thence shoots a beam, — I swear by all the heavens
  That Door shall open, if I break it in!

[In the motion to approach that Door he slips from *Mysta's* hands, and loses all vision.]

Camillus, Oh misery! So it is but the stuff of dreams!
  Yet true, because so purely beautiful!
  This vision we must try to imitate
  By a protection from the astral world,
  Such as a magic circle would effect;
  What if we reerected our old kiosks
  Which once had served a purpose similar?

Maga, Having achieved equality with us,
  You need no longer our permission ask,—
  But take it! Your initiation is your claim;
  Thereby demonstrate you are hierophants.

Camillus, [passionately], Wherefore from thee this
         sacred robe I pluck,
  Therein myself straightway to initiate!

Mysta, [imitating,] I will assume the hierophantic robe;
  We would, we will, we are, and we shall be!

    [The *Mages* sing in a minor key,]

Mages, In ages past, before the world arose,
  The Heavenly Love went out into the Deep,
  And gave itself to those that it had made;
  Oh the eternal sorrows of the Gods
  Who ruled by serving, and by death of self!

(The *Mystics* descend, from the Cave-barricade pull out the pieces belonging to their former kiosks, and reestablish them differently. Inside the Cave are found additional pieces, whereby the kiosks are all joined into one single domed sanctuary.)

TWELFTH, the SUPREME FATHER

Camillus, MAGES, obeying, we have done our best,
   And are protected from the Spheral Powers;
   But now to make the vision real is the task.
Mysta, We will do our best, and that is the divine!

[She suddenly starts, noticing underground pieces which when dug up and fitted together form a dome for the combined structure, which till now had no dome. It has no door, but a window in each panel. In a major key sing the]

Mages, The younger gods show forth their new divinity
   By resurrecting New Jerusalem
   More wisely, strongly, square and perfectly.
   Each year as bride from Heaven, a newer dome
   More gloriously surmounts fresh edifice.

(As the *Neophytes* finish the construction, they are unable to repress exclamations such as the following,]

Mystics, Divinely fair! Gracious and beautiful!
   Such dome could shelter every homing race!
   The tomb of error, cradling the divine!
   Symmetric college of divinity!

2, The Gate of Humility.

Camillus, Halt, MYSTA, our joys are premature!
   The structure gleams, but only points a void
   Like to a statue yet without a soul.
   Presences wait oblations' votive call,
   And so should we to them some gift present.
   Here is the term of all our voyages,
   Our high adventure here awaits its goal;
   Here twists the knot that ravels all the worlds;
   Here broods the dream that saves humanity,
   Can raise the dead, heal weariness and sin,

188 TWELFTH, *the* SUPREME FATHER

This is no time for caution or reserve,
But time when prudence changes to largesse.
He will be richest, who has given most;
Pilgrim, turn king in generosity. —
A boon, a gift, an offering, a pledge!

Mysta, Well said, but tell us also what to give!

Camillus, [crestfallen,] I stand rebuked, though generous the wish;
No one possession do I own, to give.

Mysta, What of your robe?

Camillus, [delighted,] Here is a prize to give,
Whose giving shall confer on me the rank of king!

(He hangs the robe over the right window, when on it appears the word *King.*)

Mysta, [with deference,] Proceed into the temple, first and best.

Camillus, When you come with me, Whisperer of Truth!

Mysta, Alas, my poverty delays my steps!

Camillus, Off with your mantle, and grow royal too!

Mysta, If I grew royal, you would cease sole rule!

Camillus, It matters not, alone I enter not.

Mysta, Salvation sunders, destiny divides!

Camillus, Sundered salvation is no destiny
For souls by social services inflamed;
Off with your cloak, reluctant bride of heaven!

(She holds to it, it tears in two, down to the hem.)

Mysta, So good, — of selfishness I stand absolved;
As gift, I had not given what was mine;
But riven now, as votive offering,
Upon the left-hand window it may hang.

(As she offers the robe to *Camillus,* he blushes.)

TWELFTH, *the SUPREME FATHER*

Camillus, I had no right to give away the robe
   By initiator loaned to shelter me; —
  Forgive me, God, the sacrilegious deed!

[He goes to the sanctuary and tries to pull it off, but his efforts fail. *Mysta* falls down in a convulsion, and then stands up raving, uttering as an oracle,)

Mysta, Mortal, beware! Thy gift has made thee king;
   Without repentance are the gifts of God;
  No less thy gifts to God! Who gave has won!

Camillus, But it was not mine! Indeed I was a thief!

Mysta, None finds the Kingdom, but he captures it
   By violence!

Camillus, Juster than God, I challenge even Him!

Mysta, His own initiator was the king!
   By proper use he made the robe his own.
   For had he not an initiator been
   He had not had the neophyte to teach.
   Its former owner only put it on
   To have his pupil tear it from his back.
   Man's bliss is to be needed, and be used,
   Predestined to be robbed and crucified.
   Now you may offer up your robe to God,
   Having in safety passed humility.

[Vague shapes of light hover around her; she bids them pass, and sits motionless. Soft strains die out in a low C.)

Camillus, Yes, yes; I have been selfish in all this;
   We thought of them as no more needing love
   And comfort, — they who gave so lavishly!
   Why can attainment not be had, without
   Giving some grief unto some holier one?
   Could I but climb without creating grief!

Mysta, [entranced,] Who speaks of MINE and THINE
               when all is God's?

Owner of all, to stewards He entrusts.
Whatever pride thou hast, employ it best
Making good use of what thy God doth lend.
Only a robe hast thou? Then elevate
It like a sacred host, as votive unto God.

Camillus, But why deprive someone of what he needs

Mysta, [entranced,] The Prophet ends, the Judge
shall now proceed.
This is the cause of grief vicarious:
No human soul can ever be saved alone,—
No child is born without a mother's pangs,—
'Rights' individual, evolution's flower,
Are but a privileged achievement rare;
But, like spoiled children, we would call them **rights**,
And scold whenever urgencies arise,
Use them as vantage-ground to cut our roots,
To undermine the ground on which we stand,
Ask 'rights' to ruin, and claiming wild
The peace protected by society,
We do our utmost to destroy the same:
The individualist is a traitor fool.
Linked unto thousands, none dare talk with God
Unless he serves, — that is what kingship means!

Camillus, My hand shall stop my mouth, as I adore!

Mysta, By service demonstrate thy royalty!

[*Camillus* helps *Mysta* hang her divided robe over the other windows, immediately sounds middle E.]

Camillus, As priest, I celebrate the sacrament
Of adoration and self-sacrifice!

3, Temptation.

(The *Mages,* with veils over their faces, are sitting by; the two tones wave up and down continuously, as an æolian harp. Suddenly, from within, are heard howls of pain, cursing, laughter.]

TWELFTH, the SUPREME FATHER

Camillus, Where none has entered in this sanctuary,
How could it have become so very full,
While we, the builders, are kept out?
Modest, we would have purified ourselves
Before we entered; — what a company!

Mysta, MYSTUS I heard!

Camillus, Come back!

Mysta, Down with the place!

Camillus, Wait till we understand how this took place
Since larger issues may thereon depend.
Might not the magic circle have been spoiled?

Mysta, [examining it,] All is well. That crew entered
from above.

Camillus, Nonsense! From heaven comes no crowd
like that!
Besides, no upper opening was left!

Mysta, Listen, no bars affect the spirit-world;
They entered not, — they were already there!
Only, invisible until the last
Protecting veil had sheltered from approach;
In every place is heaven or hell unseen.

Camillus, Then open windows, all will disappear!
Can you relieve of MYSTUS the remorse
That he turned coward by the fateful Bridge?
You are at fault, who failed to pray for him!

Mysta, [kneeling,] Now pray for me, that I forgot
those prayers!

[As they are praying, the pandemonium stops; there is heard the quiet conversation of two *Voices,*]

First Voice, You err, ORONTES, making such a noise.
Vain are desires for their former friends;
Let them come in; I wager they would fail
To recognize the place in which they stand!

TWELFTH, *the SUPREME FATHER*

Second Voice, [dulcet, unctuous, pious, jeering,] Glory to God, eternal, supreme, glory for ever, Amen!
    The waters shimmer in their Lord's delight!
    Holy, holy, holy. Lord God of Sabaoth!

Third Voice, [pitiful,] Last week once more I failed: ruined am I!

Fourth Voice, Enter, O Candidates of Light:
    This is the secret, that there is no truth!
    That's why he dies who lifts the 'veil of Truth,'
    And none returns, ashamed of his defeat!

Fifth Voice, Whom did you ever meet who had attained
    Which two good people ever did agree?
    Humanity agrees incurably!
    Where many err, what matters small mistake?
    Notice, the MAGES dare not utter word!

Sixth Voice, CAMILLUS felt the truth of what I said!

Seventh Voice, In broidered robe he felt himself a king,
    As blushing MYSTA did him reverence!

Mysta, Not true! I love your destiny, not you!

Camillus, He is no devil, for he spoke the truth!
    (Gentle laughs from within.)

Eighth Voice, Here is the revelation of the Truth!

[The *Mages* remain immovable; their wavering chant continues to waver up and down ceaselessly.]

Camillus, I did not know such vanity in me!

Ninth Voice, We will fool them to the fullness of their bent:
    Each sees and hears what holiest is in him.

Rich Mellow Man's Voice, Silently from heaven descends the Bride!

Soft Woman's Voice, Bridegroom divine, our nuptials bless!

TWELFTH, *the* SUPREME FATHER

Mysta, [furious,] Up and around! Break in!

Camillus, [sobbing,] Is nothing true?

Mysta, [to the *Mages,*] Still harping on?
   Under their veils they're laughing, I declare!
      I shall force your help!

Magus, [in great sorrow,]   Did you mean what you said?

Mysta, I challenge you, Guide of my soul!

Magus, Not even spoken word will I accept;
   Write it down!

Mysta, You know full well we have no ink!

Magus, But you have blood!

Mysta,   Could it be really true
   That the Supreme revealed is wickedness?

(From the sanctuary issue smoke, cries, curses, blows. The *Mystics* tear strips from their robes, prick their veins, and scrawl their names on the rags. Waving her challenge, cries)

Mysta, Challenge for help! I dare you to unveil!
   I shall accuse you on the Judgment Day!

Maga, Tryst I accept, to meet on Judgment Day!
   Hereby am I discharged!

(Her note ceases. From under a stone crawls a hideous scorpion who rushes to the edge of the hill, and noisily falls down into the valley.]

Magus, CAMILLUS seems repentant of his words!

Camillus, Am unrepentant, but would not lose you!

Magus, But I discharge myself! Give me your screed!
   Till Judgment Day! Then will I meet you there!

Camillus, I did not ask a tryst!

Magus, I give it then, and you shall not evade!

Camillus, I do repent!

Magus, It is too late!

Camillus, And why?

Magus, Salvation's social, not individual;
    One of you challenged, both must now proceed.

Mysta, Explain why individuals then failed!

Maga, Entrance there is for individuals
    Unto instruction, and to discipline;
    But perfect vision of divinity
    Cannot be had by any one alone,
    For reasons stated later by yourselves.

Camillus, That is evasion of the truth you are afraid.

Maga, Alas, farewells have now become our fate;
    But had it only been some other way!

Magus, CAMILLUS, you at least may yet be saved!

Camillus, [touching *Mysta,*] We swore never to part in earth or heaven;
    Or, if need be, in hell! Together we stand!

Mysta, Even to us you should yourselves explain!

Maga, Silent we stayed, not to disturb our prayers
    For you; did you not hear their pleading tone?
On your own heads your blood; released, we leave!

    (The *Mages* go, the *Mystics* weep.)

Mysta, Where men as leaders fail, the women must
    Snatch victory out of supine defeat.
    Follow, who judged yourself unfit to lead!

(She takes a stone and tries to break down a panel. It grows dark; wandering sparks crackle.)

Voice, In whose name do you knock?

Camillus, In hers and mine!

Bass Voice, If entrance you can force, why ask for it?
Camillus, Are you quite sure the path is right?
Mysta,   So far
    The road led upwards; why not upwards still?
    Here is some likely place yet unexplored;
If heav'n, we're saved; if hell, we'll save ourselves.
Camillus, Amen! Proceed!

Voice, Who tears the veil away from Truth is damned!

Mysta, Already damned are we; seek saints to fright!

Voice, It is your own best self that bars the way;
    The MAGES gone, delusions rampant here,
    Sinners yourselves, what senseless folly drives
    Intrusion into places not your own?

Camillus, Law, conscience, wisdom, — strangers to
                                 despair!

(From within, angel-rustlings and weepings, with distracted musical chimes. Irregular flashes of supernal light issue from the cracks; noises as of hammers crushing stone.)

Camillus, They batter down the Truth! Courage!
                                       Success!

Voice, [sadly,] Our duty is fulfilled; thrice-warned,
    Self-murderers, enter! Welcome unto hell!

(Thunder and lightning; a furious wind blows in the robes; darkness, mist, silence, emptiness.)

4, Residuary Specializing Self-Initiation.

[There is revealed the inside of the Sanctuary, which is empty. The *Mystics* are climbing in through the windows. They shiver with cold, and climb out again to bring in their mantles; they huddle themselves therein with despairing gestures.)

Mysta, Forgive me, O CAMILLUS, for my fatal feud
    Which alienated from us our dear Guides.

TWELFTH, *the SUPREME FATHER*

    I never dreamed those Voices could be right;
    But now I am convinced, *There is no Truth!*

Camillus, Except brute facts! Could Truth be separate
    From God? Since life is empty feeling's sound,
    Can we expect truth different from life?
    Unless indeed the only Truth could be
    Return unto material spheres of life?

Mysta, Go if you please, but I shall stay till **dawn**;
    For truth might be some mental entity
    That still might visit us in silence here.
    I am ashamed, confessing to no God!
    Though warned that sight of truth was suicide,
    I will defeat despair by blind belief!

Camillus, Onr own delusions are our own regrets;
    We might keep still about this grief supreme,
    As did the MAGES, though their eyes were sad;
    But what to our successors shall we say?
    We chose them; now admitted to the Gate,
    Warning were useless; they would not believe,
    And think us devils. I refuse to live,
    Dishonored thus! I must discover here
    What will remain of iife, with Truth destroyed!
    Although outside of us there were no Truth,
    I could live on as if it did exist!

Mysta, Let us therefore make out a catalogue
    Of what remains to us within ourselves.
    First, are six truths of our external lives:
    First are the lives of wise and noble men;
    Second, good memories in our own lives;
    Third, are the Scripture-poems of all times;
    Fourth, preparation for the change of death;
    The wise, judicious voice of conscience, **fifth**;
    Sixth is unselfishness, charity, love!

TWELFTH, the SUPREME FATHER

Camillus, Then there are six interior certainties:
    First, education and development;
    Second, the innate strength of self-respect;
    Third is celestial shine of constancy;
    Fourth, honor, brotherhood and loyalty;
    Fifth, warnings, comforts, dreams and prophecy;
    Sixth, the eleven abilities derived
    From training in this mystic discipline:
    Resisting not the sword, watching and health,
    Catholicity and discerning truth;
    Judgment, reincarnation, followed by
    Redeeming service, planning holy dreams,
    Drawing magic circles, evoking souls.
    These powers none can take away from us;
    They are our heaven!

Mysta,   This at least is ours!

Camillus, Perhaps the MAGES were not quite so wrong!

Mysta, Then twelfth, it seems to me, were to apply
    These principles in actual deeds of help.
    We will prepare ourselves to struggle with
    Our Initiators for the neophytes,
    To warn them that there is no Truth up here,
    And from Truth's ruin save our self-respect
   By treating them as we should have been helped—
    So let us plan the methods we shall use!

Camillus, A lesson shall we teach this God of Truth!
    He shall behold us fearless, kind, but frank!

Mysta, Truth will I picture, make and symbolize!

Camillus, Each shall be treated full constructively!

Mysta, I shall inspire him with creative love!

Camillus, Teach that indiscipline is the only hell!

Mysta, He shall be given outlines of his course!

TWELFTH, *the SUPREME FATHER*

Camillus, I'll organize his victory, through friends!
Mysta, He shall succeed by thinking that he can!
Camillus, Firmly shall he defy his own defeats!
Mysta, Lest he grow wild throngh sheer despair, I'll teach
    Sufficient proof of God is sanity!
Camillus, Sufficient certainty is the Shrine of Truth,
    Since, without Truth, interior strength survives.
Mysta, Good! This must be the Revelation sought!
Bankrupt we thought ourselves, yet find twelve gems
And have devised twelve god-like saving schemes,
  Not dreaming that this Truth-shrine should become
    The theatre of our divinity;
    The Truth not being some external thing
    But our achievements, and the insight won.
    Ourselves we thus have initiated here,
    By using the ideals that we dreamed.
Camillus, Now let us organize all candidates
    According unto what they should become.
    In black, the Feet-man should become a Priest;
    In azure, Ankle-men should sing as Bards;
    Green-clad, the Knee-men into Statesmen grow;
    The Thigh-man grows a Prophet, orange-clad;
    The Secrets-man, in yellow, Executioner;
    Amber, the Kidneys-man will grow a Judge.
Mysta, Crimson the sympathetic Artist grows;
    Men of the heart, in scarlet, Lovers grow;
    The purple Chest-man shows Maternal powers;
    The Shoulders-man grows Builder, clad in brown;
    The Neck-man, when a Healer, golden glows;
    Royal becomes the Brain-man, but in grey.
  Now we must learn the special prayer for each.

TWELFTH, *the* SUPREME FATHER

Camillus, Starting, we first intone the **Common Prayer,**
So-called from union of the praying minds,
Which forms its magic pow'r, that's voided by
The least distraction: — which let us eschew!

The Common Prayer

O God, O Heaven, O Self, O Righteousness,
O storied Presence, sacred Soberness,
Who better than ourselves our soul-needs know'st
Whose love for us is greater than our own,
Whose wisdom answers wisest prayers alone,
Who art the strength of all aspiring strife,
The praise, the joy of iridescent life, —
Enter amongst us, and with us remain,
While we the altar-fires of prayer maintain.

Camillus, The Grey Prayer must be offered by a Priest.

Grey Feet-Angel, Most let thy Presence be my victory,
My inspiration, joy and destiny!
(He disappears, raining down crocus blooms, with the challenge)

Mysta, The Brownish Prayer is powerless but from Bards!

Brown Ankle Angel, The waters of the sacred pool-depths stir,
That we may leave in them all thoughts that err.
[Disappears, raining down snow-drops, with the challenge-screed]

Camillus, The Red Prayer next, a Statesman's keenness brings.

Red Knee-Angel, Break not my will, but lure it, that it fuse
With thine, on Fates thou darest not refuse!
[Disappears, raining down holly-branches, with the challenge.)

Mysta, Alone from Prophets acts the Prayer that's Pink.

Pink Thigh-Angel, My urgencies prophetic so constrain

TWELFTH, the SUPREME FATHER

> They may effect what cannot be explained!

(Disappears, raining down chrysanthemums, with the challenge.]

Camillus, The Yellow Prayer is Executioner's.

Yellow Secrets-Angel, Lest I create new obstacles, suffuse
> My fluxful powers to transcendental use!

(Disappears, raining down hop-flowers, with the challenge.]

Mysta, Only from kings will act the Azure Prayer!

Azure Brain-Angel, Give me the knowledge of what is thy will
> The wish to do it, and the strength and skill!

(Disappears, raining down daffodils, with the challenge-screed.)

Camillus, The Deep-blue Prayer heals most by Healer winged.

Blue Neck-Angel, Let me accept each circumstance as best,
> As crown, as scourge, as initiating test.

(Disappears, raining down carnations, with the challenge-screed)

Mysta, The Violet Prayer must now to Heaven ascend!

Violet Shoulder-Angel, My past bring back, my present realize,
> And give me grace good future to devise!

[Disappears, raining down violets, with the challenge-screed.)

Camillus, The Purple Prayer from Mother must be born!

Purple Chest-Angel, I ask not that my duties should be changed,
> But that my attitude be rearranged!

(Disappears, raining down poppies, with the challenge-screed.)

Mysta, The Prayer that must be loved by Lovers is Green!

Green Heart-Angel, Chasten my heart, my mind coordinate,

TWELFTH, *the SUPREME FATHER*

My spirit-life build up to settled state!
(Disappears, raining down roses, with the challenge-screed.)

Camillus, The Orange Prayer by Artist must be limned!

Orange Sympathetics-Angel, The Holy Ones unto my sight reveal,
That I as initiate in Temple kneel!
[Disappears, raining down daisies, with the challenge-screed.]

Mysta, And now attend the Judge's Golden Prayer!

Golden Reins-Angel, To Wisdom's balanced poise my soul adjust,
Full kind where possible, but ever just!
Disappears, raining down golden-rod, with the challenge-screed.

Camillus, Hold fast until I close, ye Master-Lights!
(The *Angels* reappear where they stood, forming a semi-circle back and around the altar; they wave palms, reciting together,)

Angels, And when we part, do Thou with us proceed,
And all that failed shall now with us succeed;
And while we puzzle out what is thy will,
We shall be blameless if life augur ill;
Trusting through everything to see thy Face,
Tasting through all thy sacramental grace,
Feeling through all thy tender pierced Hand,
Reading through all the tidings of that Land
Where every mystery shall be unsealed,
And every man in God shall stand revealed.

Mystics, The Truth once lost we now ourselves have made;
Fused are the races born in various ways;
One Lodge supports all expert destinies!
The gods have died that we might take their place,
For God consists of *meeting of the minds!*
One for all, and all for one, evermore!

5, The Council.

Camillus, The time has come to show rebellion for
    Abandonment by God, by Truth, and Guides
    By perfecting help holier than theirs,
    Thus relegating them as obsolete.
    We have reviewed the twelve Residual Truths,
    And twelve Redeeming Plans, and specialized
    As Artist Expert in some one Degree.
    Though now our initiation is complete,
    It must begin to show itself in deeds.
    Liars are we until we demonstrate
    Ability in twelve Degrees of Truth
    Upon some human soul in need of them.
    Who shall it be?

Mysta,   MYSTUS is first, of course!

Camillus, Then my successor REGULUS I chose.

Mysta, Now to the work! This help in each Degree
    Is a re-examination of ourselves;
    A recapitulation and review
    Of all our efforts till the present time;
    Wherein, should any fail, the whole is lost!
    Remember, **one for all, and all for one!**

Camillus, Our will is good, but difficult the work,
    As we are only two for twelve Degrees
    Perfection in each one of which demands
    Twelve of the Candidates, one of each kind,
    To demonstrate each method in its flower;
    Twelve of the Mystagogues, each of one kind,
    Artist predestined in his own Degree:
    A King is expert in the First Degree;
    A Healer expert in the Second one;
    A Builder expert in the Third Degree;

TWELFTH, *the SUPREME FATHER*

    A Mother in the Fourth; Lover in Fifth;
    Artist in Sixth; and in the Seventh, Judge;
    In Eighth Degree, an Executioner;
    A Prophet in the Ninth; Statesman in Tenth;
    Eleventh, Bard; in Twelfth Degree, a Priest.
    But I a King, and you a Lover, must
    Direct the progress in each single one!

Mysta, We will do our best; that is all we can.
    The Sanctuary not having any door,
    Is safe without new magic fiery sphere.
  The windows shall be closed with these our robes
    Which shall no longer here evoke a hell,
    Because no longer empty is the shrine, —
    You know it usual empty rooms to shun,
    Especially in the dark, instinctively,
    Without suspicion of the real cause.
    In prayer we now proceed around the room,
    Exorcise, dedicate, and sanctify!

(The *Mystics* follow each other around the room in prayer, waving their arms.)

Mystics, Depart from here, all spiritual Powers!
    Unto our magic work we consecrate
    This temple as our common sanctuary;
    Depart, nor enter till our work be done!

Camillus, You shall be mistress of the magic work,
    While I direct the details of our rite;
    You take the odd, and I the even Degrees.
    You shall sit down and find our charges, while
    By writing signs, we draw them both up here.

[The *Mystics* sit down. *Mysta's* eyes are bandaged, and she speaks somnolently.]

Mysta, Just now MYSTUS is gazing at the stars,
    Beside the spring. He will not hurt himself;
    Draw hard, and he will fall upon the grass.

(*Camillus* writes on the ground '*MYSTUS.*' Breathing together they thrice call hhis name. Throug the folds in the robe on the the window appears *Mystus's* spirit, swaying sleepily and stupidly. Then he lurches towards his written name, near which he lies down upon the ground.)

Mysta, REGULUS is within the gardener's house,
　　Restlessly tossing on the wicker couch.
[They call on him in the same way; he appears and lies down.]

Mysta, For First Degree I find them both quite well.

Camillus, Of course, that is just what we might expect
　　From initiates who passed the First Degree.
　　For Second Degree Mystus is quite well;
　　But Regulus will likely be confused
　　By letter on the way from sisters sick.
　　He is going to be troubled; what is to do?

Mysta, I say, the letter shall arrive delayed,
　　Forgotten in the bag, until returns
　　The messenger; it shall arrive too late
　　To dissipate his energies from how
　　To conquer his next spiritual fruit.
　　Who will see to it?

Camillus,　　　　　Trust that to me!
　　I know what books delight the messenger.

Mysta, I pass the Third Degree.

Camillus,　　　　　　And I the Fourth.

Mysta,　　　　　　　　　The Fifth.

Camillus, For Sixth Degree the way is not so clear.
　　Last month Mystus did not succeed; he is
　　Discouraged; sleeps so deep he does not stir;
　　Before three days his period will begin;
　　Some one should watch him in the vital hours.

Mysta, To-morrow I will go, if you will go next day.

Camillus, Better exchange the order, for your strong
    Mental attack will best effect the last
    Permitted magic warning stroke.

Mysta, Let us omit examination
    In last Degrees; this is the vital one
    Where MYSTUS failed; and is too far ahead
    For REGULUS. Both need inspiring cheer:
    Let us instil into their dreaming minds
    Those sacramental prayers that we composed.
    In waking, they will find these stirring thoughts
    Haunting their fancies, working into words,
    And let them think that they invented them,—
    Which will increase their interest therein.

    (In turn the *Mystics* repeat the Color-Prayers.)

Camillus, So may they fructify within their minds
    Until they find their way upon the Mount!

6, The Theophany.

Camillus, Now, Sister, unto the attempts supreme!
    Let each in turn suggest some element
    Or aspect of divinity for every kind of soul.
    From what I heard, the vision will remain
    Only so long as we our thoughts restrain.
    Ready?

Mysta, I am!

Camillus,   Then God prosper the work!

Mysta, I see an altar standing in the midst,
    Covered with clouds of fragrant incense-fumes!

(To the surprise of the *Mystics* the thoughts they express are objectified before their eyes, and with eyes wide open with awe they continue, with increasing dignity, as they grow conscious that they are creating the divine elements.)

TWELFTH, *the SUPREME FATHER*

Camillus, Upon the altar rests a ladder tall -
    Reaching unto the centre of the dome;
    Whereon strong angels climb, and some descend.
    Intoning hymns of cadence mystical.

Mysta, Upon the altar gleam the golden bowls,
    The candles shine, the lilies ring their bells,
    The sacrament proceeds, the wine and bread
    Await the faithful, who around it kneel.

Camillus, The angels' garments tinkle as they pass,
    The Sanctus-bell initiates the feast;
    A hundred angels worship all around,
    Each bears a taper, waves a victor's palm!

Mysta, Primeval sparks arise from out the BOWL,
    Sev'n strong archangels speed the sparks' winged flight;
    Their words therein create the images
    Of what the sparks objectively shall form.

Camillus, Creation slows; and homing spirits speed,
    Hurtling along unto their end divine;
    The BOWL once emptied now begins to fill,
    Their refluent mass forms seething flux divine!

Mysta, Divine activity now simmers down;
    The gods are dreaming of creation fresh,
    While hoary Elders, harping on their harps,
    Intone the praises of creative joy!

Camillus, The seething elements begin to steam,
    The incense forms into a mystic rose,
    Whose fragrance shall intoxicate the Heavens,
    With maze of beauty, and with trance of song!

Mysta, The gentle rustling of the Spirit wakes,
    The gift of tongues descends upon the saints;
    New jewels shine upon the Elders' crowns,
    Their lyres reecho to the whispering breeze!

TWELFTH, *the* SUPREME FATHER

Camillus, Behind the Altar springs the Tree of Life,
    The Spirit rustles in its healing leaves;
  I see twelve Branches, each with different blooms,
    Twelve fruits will furnish all immortal food.

Mysta, Around the Altar circles noiselessly
    The limpid Stream of Immortality;
    The Tideless Sea around, in glassy shine
    Bears homing ships of ventures cosmical.

Camillus, Upon the Altar now appears a GLOBE,
    A sphere that mirrors all divinity:
    Fall down and worship, ere it pass away,
    Raise unto GOD immortal gratitude!

(Thunder and lightning; the Glory fades; the *Mystics* are about to withdraw their hands, one each of which had been stretched out over their respective recumbent charges, when)

7, The Revelations.

Mysta, (interrupting), A glance of recognition I demand!
(She bends over *Mystus's* hand, rubs his forehead, and speaks into his ear,)
  MYSTUS, old friend, wish me a long farewell!

Mystus, Your love inspires me like new-made wine!
    Madness celestial courses through my veins!
    I see a question in CAMILLUS's heart,
    Why oath of secrecy was not required
    In this supreme Degree, as formerly.
    The blood-writ challenge was the oath supreme,
    A witness living, part of his own self.

Mysta, Was secrecy not asked in Twelfth Degree
    Because we were ashamed there was no Truth?

Mystus, There was no need of asking secrecy,
    For Truth, consisting of the Outer Veil,
    And that its only shrine was THEATRE.

　　　　Nor you would be inclined to tell,
　　　　Nor could an outside person be convinced
　　　　Being accustomed to recite a creed!
　　　　To share in bitter controversial feuds,
　　　　And on the devil saddle heresy.
Camillus, Why windows in the sanctuary, no doors?
Mystus, There is no Truth to enter or depart;
　　　　The tragic secret never can be lost;
　　　　The windows are for prayer, and violence
　　　　Whereby alone the Kingdom is possessed.
Mysta, Have we not been abandoned by our God?
Mystus, A pupil never quite surmounts the thought
　　　　The teacher is imposing facts on him;
　　　　While who discovers, and is thus self-taught,
　　　　Never forgets, nor loses interest.
　　　　No soul is e'er abandoned by the Truth
　　　　Since he himself thereof creator is.
Camillus, What name is best for this our novel rite?
Mystus, Since this your work was genuinely good
　　　　It is not new; each year the initiates
　　　　Discover it afresh, — which makes it Truth.
　　　　Had it been set as task, you had refused;
　　　　Had it been counselled, you had questioned it.
　　　　It is the well-known council-rite:
　　　　After the monthly crisis to decide
　　　　Best use of victory or defeat,
　　　　And to prepare for next month's soul-success.
　　　　Sleep is the time most usual for this rite;
　　　　Though they that watch, or issue summons strong
　　　　From their own lips, appointing proper time,
　　　　May consciously behold some thoughtful Face.
　　　　Next is the yearly birth-day parliament,
　　　　Then, congress of divinities at birth;

TWELFTH, *the* SUPREME FATHER

    Last, meetings irregular at some vow,
    Repentance, guidance, or some sacrament.

Mysta, What here we learn not, never will we know.

Mystus, No more than this am I allowed to tell;
    But should you ever meet the proper ONE
    Who rules the Earth, and dare to ask of Him,
    Perhaps your wish may find completion full.
    Farewell! So much I gave, because your love
    Was key that opened every door in Heaven,
    And made me worthy to be so inspired;
    Such is the magic pow'r of sacred kiss.

(*Mystus* tears away the magic screed which *Mysta* had been holding to his forehead, and falls down.)

Camillus,   Oh that I had asked why GOD will not
                                     appear!

(*Mysta* then places her screed on her own forehead, and cries:)

Mysta, Oh ears that hear not, eyes that will not see!
    Is it not plain that GOD cannot appear?
    That what appears thereby cannot be GOD?
    Where two or three are gathered in one place,
    So runs the promise, not **I come** to you,
    But **there am I already!** Hard of heart!
    The Third of Persons of Divinity
    Is a **Communion of Assembled Saints.**
    Why came ye all together? Just **to form**
    The Group of which Divinity consists.
    Together, **you are God!** — and that is why
    God is love; for sans love you cannot meet,
    Or **come together.** So **it is by love**
    You came together, and discovered Him,
    Invented Him, and organized his Heaven!
    When alone, the human soul is darkened;
    Only in company she finds herself, —

God having made her with eyes, ears, mouth,
Without whose exercise she can't be sane;
While these imply existence of her like,
With whom she may commune through word and deed
Being triunity of thought, word, deed,
Not a lonely thought hanging around loose;
Sans friends her normal self is impossible.
That's why salvation is so very slow,—
By time that a companion has appeared
The first may be too old to gain the prize.
This is the epic of divinity:
One is **insanity,** two is a **pair,**
Three is a **family,** four is a **school·**
Five is a **clan,** and six is a **tribe,**
The mystic seven is a **brotherhood.**
Eight, a **society,** and nine a **lodge,**
Ten is a **church,** eleven is a **heaven,**
And twelve will represent **divinity,**
While thirteen is the **universe** entire.
Yourselves thus form the **New Jerusalem,**
Yourselves are what you dream, and seek and know!

Camillus, Come, let us prove our group-divinity:
We are the resurrection and the life!

(They stand around *Mystus*, who recovers.)

Camillus, Why found we here no statue of the Truth?

Mystus, Could God invent a form more wonderful
Than your own body? In your mirror look!
Look in the mirror of your brother's eye!

Mysta, But what becomes of GOD when I am dead?

Mystus, Do you suppose a living person could
Perceive Divinity, even granting that
Objective duty could at all exist?
The care of ultra-individual

TWELFTH, *the* SUPREME FATHER

>Divinity inheres in a certain ONE
>Whom, if you ever meet, you may consult.

Camillus, What is the dwelling-place of God?

Mystus, To save the lost, while dwelling in the hells,
>God radiates heaven. To Him Heaven is hell,
>Because so far from those who need Him most.
>Who would approach to God must downward go
>To whence perpetually our God ascends.
>This Universe is hospital of hell;
>The devil is a spirit moribund;
>The heavenly Hierarchy has naught to do
>But cure the sinful and reform the weak.
>Pity the devils, for they need your prayers!
>Perhaps to holier souls you devils seem!

Mysta, Then Heaven and hell are mingled thoroughly?

Mystus, So thoroughly that few know where they are.
>Hell looks like heav'n, until within the Gates;
Heav'n looks like hell, till closely scanned for flow'rs
>That only grow in presence of the gods,
>Or till you listen to the ringing of the bells
>Of various human signals of distress;
>These may you ever guess and recognize!

Camillus, On reaching Heav'n, may we not there remain?

Mystus, Heaven Is neither a place nor a time,
>But preordained coincidence of both;
>Even this shrine were Heaven only while
>The opportunities would sanctify.
>Heaven itself would grow a damning hell
>Were you to stay too long within its Gates.

Mysta, O that I knew why God permits the times
>Of occultation in our spirit-view!

212 TWELFTH, *the SUPREME FATHER*

Mystus, That is the grief supreme, the flaw in GOD!
  Himself thereto develops as he can;
  Therefore he too desires his creature's love;
  Greater the sinner, greater is his need,
  Greater the closeness of Divinity.
  Great sinners even may instruct the saints
  As on God's grace alone they must depend.
  The holiest saviors had their times of doubt,
  And occultation of Divinity;
  Prayer is the only safeguard of the soul!

(A bell booms; *Mystus* waves farewell, and disappears through the window.)

Mysta, Camillus, Return! Stay with us! We will
         pray for you!

7, Farewell.

(The glow on the altar becomes brighter, until it assumes the shape of a cross whose outlines are indistinct. On one knee *Camillus* advances, extends his arms, and cries,)

Camillus, At last I have discovered thee, O Truth!

Form, No, I am not the Truth!

Camillus,   Who art thou then?

Form, To thee my name is Door.
  That is as near the Truth as thou shalt come!

Camillus, Then there is Truth somewhere?

Form, Many! A different Truth for every man!
  Truth is a **screen** through which no man can look,
   The **veil** that shows the outline of his powers!
  I throw off Truths full recklessly, — too fast
   To care if they agree. **There is a Door!**
  For thee, let that suffice!

(The *Form* which has gradually become revealed extended on the Cross, closes the conversation by growing so dazzling as to make *Camillus* faint. Like a charmed bird *Mysta* approaches, kneels, extends her arms and cries,)

TWELFTH, the SUPREME FATHER 213

What then may be thy name, O scintillating FORM?
Form, I have so many names, I answer all!
   Unto each soul I have a secret name.
   In every land I dwell; from many come
   And go; I can as well be found at home.
   Many the languages that have been mine;
   Many I taught at Babel; only one
For every soul, for snakes, for birds, for flowers.
   Many I love, by many am I loved;
   But most I love my bitterest enemy.
   Most shalt thou find Me in the mirrored sphere,
   And in the human eye, a symbol of
   The Glassy Sea, in which I e'er observe
   Whatever happens in the Universe,
   Reflected in that central crystal glass.
   To some am Pilot, Shepherd, Enemy,
   But unto all their Final Destiny,
   And, in this sense, I am their HIGHER SELF!

(From the window is heard a sudden burst of harping and *Hosannahs*. The *Form* disappears, and there is heard a mysterious)

Voice, Go to the windows, whence you shall behold
   The final revelation of the Truth!

(From outside are heard pitiable cries for help.)

Cries, Save me, O God! I perish for the Truth!
   I perish, brutalized by drudgery!
   I have sinned! Am wandering in despair!
   I shame myself, and others I disgust!
   No longer will I try! I shall attempt to die!
My master forces me to shame of which I blush!
   Oh let me die! Such life is worse than death!
   I have grown blind! Repulsed by all, I starve!
   Sold into slavery, I head for hell!

Mysta and *Camillus,* [confusedly] I cannot stand this!
    I must go and save!
  Salvation I refuse, while any grieve!
Heaven were hell, while hell lacks Heaven's help!
  Heav'n were infamy, while evil rules!
  Better than see my God, god will I grow!

(Suddenly is resumed the vision of the Sanctuary which the *Mystics* had before evoked; only it grows more and more dazzling. There appear thousands of witnesses, and a sanctus bell rings. *Angels* invite the *Mystics* to take part, and point to their shoes as if, on holy ground, they should be removed. But at the renewal of the cries for help the *Mystics* cry,)

Mysta, Farewell! I cannot stay while suff'rers cry!
Camillus, I would despise myself if I remained!

(In differing directions the *Mystics* climb out through the windows, waving farewell. A disguised trap-door in the floor raises, and out come the Mages who longingly look after the departing *Mystics.*)

Maga, I told you so, that they would both succeed!
Magus, Two more are added to the heavenly hosts!
Maga, 𝔉𝔞𝔱𝔥𝔢𝔯 𝔬𝔣 𝔉𝔞𝔱𝔥𝔢𝔯𝔰 they have now become!
Magus, Saved because lost, lost because saved!
Maga, How close a shave they had from going wrong!
Magus, I trembled also, but I prayed the more!
Maga, BROTHER, I shall feel lonely sans their cares!
Magus, I too! But MYSTUS still awaits our help;
  I feel ashamed we lost that kindly boy.
Maga. He is not lost, he *shall* not fail again!
Magus, How can we ever thank our GOD enough?
Both, Glory to God the Most High, supreme and eternal
  Glory for ever and ever, Amen!

Questions to be Answered in Writing 🖉 12

Not to be answered all at once, but each on the indicated day of the month, overlapping from 22nd to 22nd.

The ideal time to study this Degree alone is in March to April If the whole series is to be taken, it is best to begin on March 22 But the first 22nd after you hear of these Degrees is the time Providence has set for *your* beginning; *anything* ranks delay.

DAY 22, Read and copy the Degree, and memorize your favorite selections therefrom, and record them.

Day 23, What are the spiritual destinies of the twelve character-classes?

Day 24, Memorize and reproduce the *Common Prayer*, and the *Color-prayers*.

Day 25, Tell about the monthly Soul-council.

Day 26, Learn the names of the groups of different numbers of people.

Day 27, What one thing do you think the world most needs for salvation?

Day 28, What was the peculiarity of the Temple built on the mountain-peak; and what did it mean?

Day 29, How did the demons enter into the sanctuary? Explain its significance.

Day 30, What proofs did the devils advance that there was no Truth, and that the Supreme was wicked?

Day 1, If all truth was lost, what would still remain? (Read Jean Ingelow's sonnet on *Principle*.)

Day 2, Describe and explain the Theophany.

Day 3, Tell of the World Ruler, and his influence.

Day 4, What is God's supreme grief?

Practical Experiments to be Reported 🖋 12

Day 6, Make a list of famous people who thought that they had found the Truth.

Day 7, Compare their views, and note where they disagreed.

Day 8, Note their points of agreement, and draw your own conclusions.

Day 9, Repeat the experiment with people of your acquaintance, and so direct your acquaintance.

Day 10, Read Guthrie's *Spiritual Message of Literature*, and Gœthe's *Faust* for truth-definitions.

Day 11, Collect all the definitions of Truth available to you in your nearest library.

Day 12, Make up your own definition of **Truth**.

Day 13, Study how far this new Truth-definition would compel changes in your manner of life.

Day 14, Practise the changes, and note results.

Day 15, Observe and record the difference of feeling produced by being in groups of 2, 3, 4, 5, 6, 7, 8, 9, 10, 11 and 12 people. Which do you prefer, and why?

Day 16, To a meeting at your house invite such that you feel the Divine Presence. Record results.

Day 17, Try to grow conscious of your own monthly soul-council, which is held a few days before the beginning of your monthly vitality period.

Day 18, Read all the Theophanies accessible, especially the biblical ones.

Day 19, Seek one yourself, and write it out, if possible in poetry.

After reviewing this Degree, review also all the Twelve, and invoke Wisdom to sum up what you have gained from them. If this is accepted, you may apply for *Interior Membership*.